Aspire To Your Greatness!

By

Adrian Jefferson Chofor
#1 International Best-Selling Author

RHG | MEDIA PRODUCTIONS™

ACKNOWLEDGEMENTS

I believe in the power of gratitude and importance of saying, 'please' and 'thank you". On this journey as a first-time author I uttered those words very often, and I hope that with any additional publications I plan to publish one day, I have humility and demonstrate gratitude to those that have supported me.

I am deeply grateful to my editor, mentor, and cheerleader, Rebecca Hall Gruyter. Thank you for taking my calls and helping me to be open and vulnerable. I do not think this book would have been published without your support and guidance.

Special thanks, to my husband, Julius. In your own life journey and example, I see the importance of family, perseverance, and sacrifice. You work tirelessly for your family and give generously to so many. I know you don't always want to share your wife's time with so many people, so I want to express my deepest gratitude for being selfless and supporting my time in doing the work I am passionate about, including writing this book.

As a busy mother with young children, I need to thank my beautiful children, Julian and Jeneh. Mommy loves you more than you will ever know! I am grateful that you allowed me to work without interruption at times when you really wanted my attention. I am so blessed to have you both be in my life. You are my pride and joy!

My journey with you began on a slippery slope and although at times the road looked like a dead-end street, our journey showed me that the power of love and forgiveness will always prevail. I am so happy that you are in my life and proud to call you my best friend. I love you, Mother.

I learned some of life's most important lessons from you and with profound thanks, I must mention a man that made the biggest impact in my life, my Dad. I learned it was more important to have character and be known as a person of principle, than to be well-liked. You taught me the importance of hard-work, discipline, and determination. I miss you.

Most of all, I thank Jehovah God for giving me a foundation of love, hope, and forgiveness. Thank you for never abandoning me even when I strayed wayward and there was no one there to comfort me, YOU did. Thank you for hearing my prayers, holding me up when I thought I was sure to fall, never letting me down. I am forever grateful to YOU and everything that you have done for me and continue to do for me.

I know I have missed so many others, that were with me on this journey and I would like to thank you all for your friendship, encouragement, and support and I look forward to learning and growing with you as we continue on this journey together.

Table of Contents

INTRODUCTION

"When you let your own light shine, you unconsciously give others permission to do the same."
– Marianne Williamson

Throughout my life, whenever I faced my darkest days and struggled with my insecurities, fears, and feelings of inadequacy, my mind would recall a life defining moment for me.

In June 1988, I was a tall, gangly fourteen-year-old brown skinned girl, with long limbs, big feet, large hands, and teeth so large, they could barely be contained in a mouth that didn't like to be opened because being heard meant being noticed. I learned that speaking up at home only meant trouble and talking at school only brought more trouble. It was best to remain quiet, hidden in the background, or behind my older siblings.

I was never fond of the warmer months of the year because of my 'hyper-sweating' condition, known as Hyperhidrosis. This condition would cause my 'cold' hands to drip with perspiration and embarrassing sweat rings staining my clothes. As a teenage girl, becoming more image conscious, hoping to look more desirable and pretty this was not the image I wanted. My anxiety drove me to try to satisfy my insatiable sweet tooth by eating countless doughnuts, copious amounts of chocolate, and stacks of my-then-favorite snack, called Twinkies to comfort me as the sweat rolled down my back and legs. My indulgence in sweets resulted in moderate to severe facial acne and hyperpigmentation. I would wear heavy cream make-up foundation to hide the scars and even my blemished complexion. My love affair with make-up would start early, but so did my dread fear of standing out, but something changed as I approached the day of my junior high school graduation.

"I want to feel pretty!" I exclaimed to no one in particular.

I had dragged my father into one of those frou-frou stores at the local Mall with tons of tulle, satin, and poofy gowns. He had as much enthusiasm as deep-sea diver stranded in a desert at high noon. He suppressed several yawns warily watching me race around the store peering through racks of brightly colored dresses. The salesgirls in the shop didn't offer much help and I remember a feeling of hopelessness, until the sales manager approached my father. I could not hear what they were saying to one another, but I watched a lot of heading nodding and gesturing and then the most reassuring thing happened…my father smiled. They both turned towards me, hiding behind a rack of clothes clutching a brightly colored print dress two sizes too small for me, and gestured for me to join them. The sales lady removed the dress from damp hands, looked over at my Dad with a smile, and then led me to the back of the store to a dressing room. Within one hour of trying on some of the most beautiful dresses that seemed to magically appear from the hands of the patient saleslady…I found the dress! It was a gorgeous black, off-the shoulder, knee-length dress with a cinched waist. The dress was simply stunning! When I wore it with black heels and jewelry, I not only felt like a grownup, but like a beautiful young woman for the first time in my life.

I strode into the auditorium that day without a care in the world—I felt pretty! I received so many compliments that day! Many of the people that had never noticed me before, other than being the tall, athletic girl took note and told me how beautiful I looked. **I remember after the graduation ceremony, I ran up to my Father and thanked him for helping me look so pretty. "No, you ARE pretty, baby girl!" and then he added the words, I shall never forget, "Just let your light shine…let your light shine", he smiled broadly, "let your light shine," he said again with a twinkle in his eyes.** He had a habit of repeating himself when he wanted to make a point and this was not lost on me. In that moment, I *felt* beautiful, learning a profound lesson; when my feelings about myself changed, then how others viewed me also changed. I had not allowed my light to shine before because subconsciously, I didn't believe my light had any value and others were much better at shining, standing out, and being seen than me. I am so thankful I learned how wrong I was in my thinking and received this powerful lesson in my younger years.

I continued to believe those powerful words in the years that followed, including those bleak times when I was homeless and felt betrayed by family. Many times, when I wiped tears and covered bruised from my mother's beatings. The words helped me when I almost lost a well-paying job early in my career and later because of my 'friends'. I clung desperately to those words when I almost lost my child and felt betrayed by the healthcare system. **Through the difficult periods of my life, I knew that I had to let my light shine and not focus on the darkness.** I lost my dear father to cancer on April 3, 2016. His light has not extinguished because of the indelible mark he has left on all of his children, grandchildren, and great-grandchildren. **The most powerful revelation I have had about my father's loving words is that when I let my light shine, I will attract others like me, that are shining and we are making a path for others to come through the darkness. I look forward to shining with you as you Aspire to Your Greatness!**

My desire in writing this book is to authentically share my journey of overcoming and stepping into my vision, dream and purpose (my greatness). In doing so, I will be pulling back the curtain and sharing with you each step along the way that I discovered to support and help you aspire and step into your greatness. I've

discovered, aspiring to your greatness comes down to your choices, I hope in sharing my journey you will be inspired to choose to step into your Greatness and **SHINE!** As the world needs you, your gifts, talents, and abilities. Be willing to Aspire to Your Greatness!

CHAPTER 1 - LIFE'S NOT FAIR

"Congratulations! She's a BIG, healthy girl!" The doctor exclaimed, as I wailed when I was born. I was a robust baby weighing a whopping ten pounds and ten ounces at birth! My cries bellowed through the delivery room as I announced my arrival and raised my fists in the air.

'Let's name her Wanda' suggested my Dad, but my mother had already decided on a strong yet feminine name: **Adrian Quintina**. She intentionally ended the spelling of my first name with **"an"** which is the commonly accepted masculine spelling. My mother rejected the feminine spelling of **-en** because she didn't like how it appeared in print. Its Latin origin derives from the Adriatic Sea and it means *'Water'*. In German, it means *'Dark'* and *'Rich'*. I was told as a baby I would love to be bathed. I loved to be in water; swimming, sitting on a beach, staring at it from a distance. I have always felt a strong connection to water. When I think of its German origin, I think of my brown skin which some would consider dark and although I am not materially wealthy, I am rich in spirit. My middle name Quintina means *'Fifth Born Girl'* because I am the fifth child of my parents. My Parents gave me the gift of a powerful name.

My arrival was not met with enthusiasm by my parents, a young couple in their twenties that already had four children. Thus we were barely making ends meet on my Dad's salary. I was born in New York City, in the borough of Queens in an area known as Far Rockaway. We lived in the Ocean Bay apartments, then known as the Edgemere housing projects, a 24-building development that housed nearly 4,000 low-income families. The area was rapidly declining into a crime-ridden, drug-infested place and caused my father to fear for the safety of his family. He moved his family to Staten Island, the southernmost borough in New York City. It was so different from the other boroughs with its sleepy, small-town feel. Our family settled in the middle-class suburb of Arden Heights on the south shore of Staten Island. The community we lived in was predominately Italian, Jewish, and Irish. I always felt out of place, like I didn't belong in my own skin, in my family, and in my community. I was an outsider that was always looking in. This affected my outlook and my self-worth. I had to learn a lesson in standing up for myself and self-worth at a young age.

STICKS AND STONES

In the neighborhood I grew up there was a sixteen-acre park where all the residents could enjoy the playgrounds, tennis and basketball courts, pools, and baseball field. My siblings and I used to love going to that park to play. My athletic brothers would play football, baseball, and basketball with the neighborhood kids while I would play at one of the three playgrounds with slides, jungle gyms, and tire swings. One day, when I was seven years old, I decided to play on the wooden structure while my older brothers played football in a field nearby. Usually there are other kids my age to play with at the playground, but on this day, I was alone except for some older kids. At first, they didn't seem to mind my presence as I played around the structures. But then, the oldest looking one yelled, 'Hey nigger! Get outta here!' I knew instinctively that was not a good word, but no one had ever directed it to me and my instant reaction was to freeze. The other kids snickered as the older boy rose up and repeated himself, this time a little louder and with more malice. This time it had its intended effect and I began to cry. **I ran home all by myself as fast as my legs could carry me with hot tears spilling down my face.** I was angry and afraid. Before I could reach my front door, I ran into my friend, Trey. Also 6 years old…and a tall, lanky kid like me and one of the few African-American kids in the neighborhood.

"What's wrong, Adrian? What happened?" he inquired.

"Nothing!" I sniffled back. Why was I lying?

"Why are you crying?" Trey shot back with an accusing look.

"I dunno." I replied with my eyes directed at my worn shoes.

Trey rolls his eyes and playful taps me on my shoulder and then asks again, "Tell me what happened! Somebody do something to you? Come on, what's going on?"

It was then that I told him what had happened and the tears started to fall again. Trey's face looked pained when I repeated the word, but then shrugged and asked me, "Did you tell your brothers?'" In my distress, I left them playing the park and ran home without even telling them that I had left. "Oh no! I have to go back! When they realize I am not there, they are going to look for me, I gotta go back!'" Trey decided to accompany back to the park, but it was the walk back that made the difference…

"Don't let them get to you" Trey said calmly as we walked together to the park.

"Huh? Aren't you mad?" I asked

"Well, a little, but you can't let people get to you. C'mon, look at where we're at. Don't let them get to you. If they see that they are getting you then they will always try to use that against you." Trey held my gaze when he said those words to let them penetrate and then added, 'you know you are better than them!'

Well, that was just the salve I needed soothe my wounded pride.

That experience and Trey's words of wisdom taught me one of the most valuable lessons I have learned in my life. **It helped me to appreciate that we cannot control the actions of others, but we can control how react and not let others take way our self-respect or diminish our self-worth.**

THE UGLY DUCKLING

Are you familiar with the story of the '*The Ugly Duckling*', the story by Hans Christian Andersen? To help you recall, it is a story about a hatchling that looked very different from the other ducklings. He was mistreated because of his looks and made to feel less than adequate. He searched for a place where he could find acceptance, but nobody wanted him around them and would tease him mercilessly. He would look up into the sky and gaze at all the beautiful swans wishing to look like them. He endures a torturous winter of cold weather, rejections, and loneliness. By spring, the 'duckling' now fully matured, unable to endure a life of solitude decides to throw himself at the mercy of the flock of swans that he admires, expecting cruel rejection and teasing. To his surprise, the swans welcome and accept him to the flock. He then notices by looking at his reflection in the water that he has become one of them. He has finally found the acceptance he has always craved.

I was considered a late bloomer intellectually and in physical attractiveness. My second-grade teacher would single me out and make comments about how I 'held up' the class because of inability to keep up with the lessons. It was sheer torture to go to school and be confronted with her patronizing glare. She never once asked me why I couldn't stay focused on a lesson or why I stared out of the window. She would allow some of the kids to cruelly taunt me because I would stutter when it was my turn to read aloud. The truth is, I could read better than all of them, but anxiety and fear would make my jaw tighten and lips would not move. I would be reading beautifully in my mind, but the words that spilled from my mouth were garbled.

"Adrian, you had better learn how to play sports!" she would say in exasperation.

I would try to fight back the tears that were forming in the corner of my eyes, but it was no use, they would spill down and race down my face meeting like old friends at my chin. Some of the other kids would look away to protect themselves from their own discomfort and awkwardness of the situation. Others would tease me by holding up fists to their eyes and pretending to be crying themselves.

As difficult as the school environment was, it was the only place that I could go to escape the horrors that I faced at home. I did everything in my power to keep quiet, stay hidden, and be invisible. Dinner time was a joyous occasion in some homes. For me, it meant trying to get through a meal without being noticed. That rarely happened because it was the favorite time of the Boss, my mother, as she says my Father would refer to her, would hold court. She was the judge and jury. She was the warden. I was not her favorite and usually an easy mark at seven years old. If I didn't get a beating for a minor offense before dinner, I was most certain to get one after. Then, I had to clean the kitchen; wash and dry dishes and put them away. Then I had to clean appliances and counter tops, sweep the floor and clean the dining room before going to bed. If it was not spotless, I would be dragged out of bed and marched downstairs to clean everything until it met her standards and passed her inspection. Sometimes, I would literally be out of my mind with exhaustion and could not respond quickly enough to her line of questioning because I was not fully awake….."A-DRI-an! Didn't I say I didn't want ANY grease on this stove?" she would have my face inches from the stove, pointing to a greasy spot on the stove.

"Uh-huh." I would respond because my seven-year old head not woken up.

Boom! A slap upside the head. That helped bring me back to reality. I would clean the offensive markings from the stove. Pray that nothing else was out of order and go back to the only safe place I had: my dreams, my bed, my sleep.

I would be plagued with headaches and migraines from the age of seven until my mid-twenties, I believe was due to the angst, pain, and effort of repressing my voice. I felt like the ugly duckling that did not fit in anywhere. The helpless little bird would gaze into the sky, like me, but the difference is I would be looking at the airplanes flying overhead. **I would pretend I was on one of them and going to a beautiful, glamorous place where I would be accepted and loved.**

GOODBYE TO ANGER'S LITTLE SISTER

A mother is usually described as loving, nurturing, comforting, and supportive. They are the backbone of the family and usually, the glue that holds it together. My mother from childhood would be described as combative, dismissive, highly critical, and extremely controlling. She played favorites amongst her six children and would play them against one another. My second oldest brother and I were the targets of her aggression and unprompted acidic attacks. Her attacks were used to lethally diminish our self-confidence. One of her methods to undermine me was by body shaming. I was *'too tall'*, *'too wild'*, *'my butt too big'*, *'my chest too small'*, *'your feet too big'*. She would make scathing remarks about the way I walked and talked. I became more and more self-conscious about my height and weight. Everything I did was subject to her disapproving scrutiny and usually resulted in beatings I received almost daily with a

16" x 8" wooden paddle ball racquet. My mother was a strong woman, with a backhand that could rival

Serena William's, with each hit she inflicted I thought I would faint from the pain.

I remember one horrible day in 1987. I was thirteen years old and at this time it was popular to wear name and initial jewelry in my area. Many women and girls had gold necklaces or bracelets with their name. A gold ring usually had the initial of the first name of the wearer. My mother had a beautiful gold ring with the cursive letter 'J' that I admired. I knew if asked her to wear it, she would not only tell me absolutely not, but her response would come with a verbal put-down. This did not stop me from wanting to wear the ring, so I devised a plan to get it and wear it on a half-day of school. I would wait for her to leave for work, retrieve it from her belongings, wear it to school and put it back before she got home. The plan went well until I tried the ring on. It was several sizes too big for me! What would I do? Aha! I came up with the idea to wind scotch tape around it several times making a 'poor girls ring guard' to make the ring fit. The plan worked! Off to school I went and showed off *my* beautiful ring that stood for my last name, Jefferson. On the way home, I decided to take the ring off and put it in my school bag because I didn't want any of my siblings to see me wearing it and tell her. I was the first person to arrive home. Whew! I can put the ring back and no one will see me do it. Oh no! The ring was GONE! I saw my life flash before my eyes. I panicked and searched the house. Then I heard the key in the lock. I tried to control my breathing and act nonchalant when one of my siblings walked through the door, but it wasn't any of them – it was HER! My heart sank and I prayed she would not notice her ring was missing. But, not only did she know her ring was not in the house, she knew I had lost it because it was in her hand! She calmly asked me if I had seen her ring. I lied to try to save my hide and said I hadn't seen it. She then opened her hand and showed it to me. It was laying in between the screen and front doors. It must have fallen out of my bag when I got the keys to enter into the house.

She then grabbed her paddle ball racquet and beat me again and again. *The. pain. was. unbearable.* She threatened me not to yell or scream because she didn't want the neighbors to know she was beating me. She beat me until she was too tired to lift her arm and catch her breath. Then she calmly walked away from me leaving me laying there. It took several moments to gather the strength to try to move. My wrists were swollen from arms flailing during the beat instinctively trying to block all the hits. She made sure to hit them even harder because she always told me to keep my hands from 'back there' when she gave me a beating. My thighs, buttocks, arms, and hands had enormous welts. It took several days to walk and sit without feeling pain. **The swelling went down within days as well, but the internal damage was done. I had never felt so unwanted and unloved. The beatings lasted until I was sixteen years old,** but the verbal putdowns lasted well into my twenties.

At the age of eighteen, I finally left home, escaping the beatings and verbal assaults. The physical scars healed, but the years of dismissive behavior and emotional detachment from my mother eroded my self-esteem leaving me with intense feelings of uncertainty and self-doubt. I was hypervigilant and defensive, always ready to stand my ground against any perceived offense. Maltreatment and abuse had aroused so much anger in me over the years that I suffered from crippling migraines and depression. Soon after I left home, anger abandoned me and left its little sister, bitterness in its place.

The smoldering resentment insidiously built up a wall in me not allowing me to connect or trust anyone. My strong sense of justice would not let me forget all the 'wrongs.' I thought if I allowed myself to *forget*, then I was letting her win, and I would be considered weak. Most of my thoughts were consumed with revenge as I would ruminate on my past painful experiences. I would talk, no, I would rage to whoever was in ear shot about my misfortune… especially if I had been drinking. The drinking helped to remember, sometimes it helped to forget, but it never helped me to heal. I had to learn that through the power of forgiveness. Forgiveness helped me to refocus my energy on building the future I wanted and not helplessly holding on to the past that I couldn't change. The most painful wounds are usually the ones that you cannot see and if allowed to fester, they can cause the most damage. In the case of a wound, the deeper it is, the best course of action is to seek professional help to have it looked at for treatment. I sought out professional help to support me in my healing process. In my early twenties, I started on a personal journey to forgiveness. When I truly embraced forgiveness, and fully let go of the things that made me feel 'powerless,' I began to feel **'powerFUL'** and re-energized. My mental health and outlook improved. I didn't have to pretend I was OK, I felt 'OK.' I felt empowered. The next chapter will share lessons I discover on my journey of shifting from feeling angry to powerful.

Aspire To Your Greatness!

1. **You Are Valuable.** No matter what those around you see and say, you have great value and are worthy of love and respect.

2. **Stand In Your Truth.** Don't let others get to you; or decide who you are. Stand in your truth. Remember…. Don't let them get to you.

3. **You Are Beautifully and Wonderfully Made.** You are not an ugly duckling…but truly beautifully and wonderfully made. Sometimes you just need to find a new group or circle that recognizes your beauty.

4. **Be Willing to Release the 'Wrongs.'** Anger, bitterness, and resentment actually end up hurting you in the end and holding you back. Be willing to release the 'wrongs' so you can soar.

5. **Forgive.** Forgiveness isn't forgetting or pretending it didn't happen. It's releasing the hold of pain and anger that is only hurting you. Be willing to free yourself from the past so you can move forward. This will allow you to build a powerful and beautiful future starting now.

CHAPTER 2 – THE WILDFLOWER

"What up, baby? Where ya going, huh?"

I kept my eyes partially shut from fatigue and the prayer that the intrusive voice would go away. The swaying rhythm of the subway train was a blessing and a curse as it lulled me to sleep, but I had to remain vigilant because danger crouches in every corner for a young woman traveling at 2am in the morning on the perilous trains of New York City.

"You sho' is fine. What's your name?"

I pulled my hoodie tighter over my head and kept my eyes shut hoping the man would get the message. He had a strong, husky voice of a man over forty with enough sense to know he was approaching a girl of 18, young enough to be his daughter. He sat down next to me and leaned in close. I could smell the liquor on his breath and the faint smell of cigarettes and sweat emanated from his shirt.

"You gonna tell me yo' name?" he asked and gently placed his hand on my thigh. My eyes popped open! Ugh! The glare of the train's fluorescent lighting struck me with the force of a pail of water being thrown in my face. I immediately squinted to get a look at the perpetrator as I slapped his hand off my leg. He raised his hands in the air and shrugged his shoulders as if to say – what's your problem? He then chuckled and said, "look, I jus' asked for yo name.

What's wrong? You don't wanna talk to me?" I looked around the subway car and there was young Hispanic guy that looked more interested in fixing the tape that had unwound in his Walkman than in my situation. The other two individuals were guys that looked as creepy as the one that was trying to make a move on me. The train screeched into the next station and I knew I had to make my move to get off the train.

I grabbed my bag to make a dash out of the train when the doors opened when I felt a hand grab my arm. My mind raced with so many thoughts in that moment. I cannot recall what the man said in that moment because my only reaction was to fight. Fight. Fight with everything I had and then run. I swung around, dropped my bag, and kicked him as hard as I could. I heard him howl with pain before I landed a couple of blows to his head as he charged for me. I was quicker than him. I grabbed my bag and ran out of the train, the doors almost catching my heel. I ran across the platform onto the train heading in the opposite direction. My heart was racing. My head was pounding. My body was exhausted. All I wanted to do was cry and that is what I did. The tears trickled down my face slowly at first, but when the train pulled out of the station and entered the tunnel, my body overcome with exhaustion and my spirit broken by the shame of my situation released a flood of tears.

Heave. Sob. Heave. Sob. Minutes passed. The train makes it way south retracing the direction I have come from. It was then that I noticed an older woman sitting across me. Her face looked as if she had weathered many storms in her own life. She did not say a word. She held my eyes for a moment, closed them and raised her head heavenward before releasing a *deep* sigh. The sigh. What was it supposed to mean? Did it signify something? Did it mean she was able to relate to my struggle? Did she understand I had just been assaulted? Did she feel pity for me as she watched me cry? Or was she just a tired worker on her way home? In that moment, I felt more alone than I had ever been. Young. Homeless. Afraid. How had my life come to this?

When I moved in with my brother in his basement apartment in Queens after leaving my parent's house in Staten Island. The stern warning that I was *on my own* mattered very little to me at 18 years old. I felt liberated. The first few months were glorious. I didn't see the dark clouds on the horizon. Had it just been four Months?

WAKE UP CALL

In 1993, America was experiencing a recession. The job market was very competitive. It was a challenging market for a recent high-school graduate with a few years of work experience from past internships, but I was still confident I would find work. Weeks stretched into months of unemployment. One day, my brother announced the landlord had sold the property he was renting and he was planning to move in with his then-girlfriend. I could barely recover from that announcement when he said we needed to leave in *two weeks*. We need to leave? In two weeks? Where was I going to go? My father worked for many years with IBM and they had relocated him to Austin, Texas around the time I moved out. Let's not forget my mother's stern warning that I was on my own when I moved out and that I was not welcome in *her* new house. I was on my own. Ok, got it. I shook that thought out of my head. I quickly thought about all my contacts and started making calls.

A few days on the couch here, a spare room there, a makeshift bed on the floor other times. Nothing permanent. Travel light. Don't complain. Say thank you and stay out of their way, especially the men. I developed my own 'survivor' rules:

1) If the man of the house or any man living in that house starts to look at you differently when your friend is not around – GO! No goodbyes. Get out! Trouble was lurking. I would call her and tell her I found another place to stay.

2) I would not sleep laying down. I had to be propped up against the wall. Better to be safe than sorry, although many mornings I found myself laying on my side.

3)Do not use the bathroom before or after everyone else and take no more than five minutes.

4)Do not eat their food and if offered, eat very little. I learned that if you didn't eat much, people didn't consider you to be a burden, and let you stay with them longer.

5) Clean underwear and socks were always a blessing.

6) Run out of toothpaste, 'no problem mon' just get a chewing stick or 'wis'. A Jamaican friend I knew shared with me the benefits of chewing on a stick that cleaned and whitened your teeth. Very affordable too.

7) Sleep with cash on you. Always on you.

When I couldn't find a place to 'crash'. There was a couple of times I spent the night on the subway. I learned sleeping on the train is better in the afternoon, less risk of being attacked. The only individuals interested in the homeless are the transit police.

As my situation grew increasingly dire, I grew more and more despondent, but I felt safer on the street than in a shelter. **There were times I was too ashamed to go on job interviews because I did not have the right attire or was not clean. Yet, I needed work! I needed a place to live! No one wanted a 'freeloader' on their couch. I was exhausted, ashamed, and nearly broken. Unwanted and unloved. I was in the bloom of my youth like a fresh flower, beautiful with so much potential, and yet I felt as unwanted as a weed on a manicured lawn. A weed to be picked and cast aside.** Was I a weed or something else? I wished to be that beautiful flower and I had to convince myself that I was. I decided and claimed that I *a wildflower.* They are resilient, grow in any season and are known for adapting to the harshest conditions to survive. I was like a wildflower adapting to all the withering heat and blustery cold like situations that life handed me. *I was a survivor.* **Like a wildflower penetrating through concrete and bursting forth in bloom, I would do the same by rising out of my situation. I may be gentle, but like a wildflower in beautiful resiliency and power, nothing can stop me from flourishing. I would not only survive. I would thrive.**

Thoughts and words have power. I whispered, spoke, prayed and cried out until God answered. Word about my situation reached my father in Texas, and he sent me a ticket to come and live with him and my mother. God answered my prayers, loves me and I had to conclude that He has an amazing sense of humor. I was going to live under the same roof of the woman that tormented me for most of my childhood in a state that was known for cowboys, over-sized everything, and love for everything country.

GOING TO THE LONE STAR STATE

On July 4, 1993 when most of America was celebrating their independence, I felt like I had just lost mine. Any resolve I had to be strong, dissolved with the first blast of the heavy, hot, humid Austin summer heat. I thought part of my face had melted off when I stepped out of the airport to wait at the Arrival gates for my parents to pick me up curbside. Then I spotted my Father's blue Lincoln. I took a deep breath. "Ok, girl, you can do this" I said to myself before I caught myself sighing like that old woman on the subway in New York. I finally understood her sigh. It's a sigh reminding yourself that you are not alone and you can do this!

Oh, how I missed New York already. I wanted to run back into the airport demanding a return to the place that I loved and knew, but I was stuck in Podunk Ville. I lamented my situation. How was a girl like *me* to survive?

My Dad, savior, and forever knight, was the first one hopping out of the car. He rushed up to me to give me to give me a big hug. I loved hugging my Dad because his hugs weren't perfunctory. He would hold me tight, like it was the final time we would see each other, and tell me how much he missed me. **I just wanted to be loved. I missed him. He always made me feel special.** I always felt that he was torn in his allegiance to me and my mother. She would always win. My younger brother and mother remained in the car. When I got in it, I understood why. The air conditioner roared full blast turning the car into a cool oasis from the brutal Texas heat.

"Those britches sure look tight" she exclaimed coolly when I got into the car. Hmmm, maybe the air conditioner wasn't the only thing keeping the temperatures frigid in the car.

Was this her only greeting for me? And…who in the heck says *britches* in 1993?

She must have been reading my mind because she then said, "Don't even think you are wearing those pants in my house!"

I wish she would have asked me why I had lost weight since leaving her house or why was I wearing those hand-me-down pants. I tried to shrug off her remarks and look outside of the window gazing upon my new city. A place I didn't want to live in. Why, God, why? Don't cry. Don't sweat. Aw man, even in this frigid icebox of a car, I am sweating.

We pull into the driveway of a beautiful, white palatial home. My Father is excited to give me a tour of the exquisite 5-bedroom home with a study, guest bedroom, and sitting room. A sitting room. I was homeless and three people are living in this palace. My Mother calls out to my Father from the master bedroom and tells him to *send* me to her. I feel like I have just been summoned by the warden of San Quentin penitentiary. I walk pensively into the massive space trying not to gawk at the sheer size. I was homeless sleeping on floors and my parents had a bedroom bigger than the average size apartment in New York.

"Do you hear me talking to you?"

You mean at me? Uh, yeah. "Yes, I hear you" I nod as I tell her I am listening.

"You have six months to be in *my house*! I don't care if you are on the street! Six months. That's it!" she said with venom dripping from each word of her pronouncement.

"I WILL SMACK THAT SMIRK OFF YOUR FACE!"

What? Did I smirk? Standing in her cavernous room as she told me that I have six months to stay in her house or I will be on the street. In that moment I felt more strongly than I ever had. I felt invincible. I would survive no matter what! No wonder she quickly dismissed me soon after.

The next day I looked for work and landed a job at a retail store in a little over two miles away. Since I did not have a car, I would have to walk a little over two miles each day in the summer Texas heat, but it was worth it. I was earning a paycheck. Each paycheck brought me closer to independence. A few months later I found a job working in a daycare and then in November 1993 I was hired by IBM to be an administrative specialist. I was thrilled! My Father would gloatingly say, "your Mother applied for jobs at IBM and never got in! Look at you!" and then laugh as he shook his head. **I laughed and shook my head too because for a moment I thought my situation was hopeless and then God laughed and said, "No, my child, I have bigger plans for you".**

Within six months, I had my own apartment and car. Me! I did it. I moved out of my parents' home. It felt good, but it wasn't great. Living in Texas for me was like a Martian living on Earth, I felt out of place. For example, I finally took up the offer to join my co-workers for a night out for dancing and drinks. They ALL swore it would be fun. After work, we all met up at one of their houses and to get ready. As you know everything is bigger in Texas and apparently, that includes hair. They sprayed on obscene amounts of hair spray to keep it all UP and OUT. And the clothes, let's just stay we had a difference in styles of clothing. I wore a loose cotton Benetton shirt with GAP jeans and sneakers and they wore jeans so tight they could cut off circulation and so stiff they could stand up by themselves. Um, I like belts, but the buckles I like are usually the size of a matchbox, but theirs were the sizes of dinner plates.

After dressing, we headed out to the party…first we headed down Interstate 35, then exited to a small town, and unto a small road that ran through that town. After a series of turns unto smaller, more-isolated roads we were in the middle of nowhere in pitch darkness. Now, I have seen too many CSI, Law & Order and 48-hour episodes not to get nervous. I was the only person of color in the car and everybody that has seen horror movies knows we are always the first to die! My heartbeat was racing and my palms were sweating but before I knew it I started to *hear* the first strains of music. It sounded like country music. Then, I saw the lights on the horizon. As we drove up to the place, I could make out it was a BARN. Inside people are do-see-do'in and boot scootin' to the music of the country band playing on hay bales in the front. First, I don't boot scoot…I could dance the 'electric slide' but wasn't familiar with country line dancing. At some point during the night, I made the resolve to return home. No, not to my one-bedroom apartment in Round Rock, a suburb north of Austin, but 'home', my hometown; New York. I was tired of feeling like a fish out of water. After two years of living in the Texas, I made plans to return to my New York and start again. **This time I didn't plan to leave it unless I left on my own terms. In June 1995, I left and never looked back. No matter where you are or have been, you can build your escape plan and step powerfully into your future!**

Aspire to Your Greatness!

1. **Declare who you are.** Words matter and what matters most is what you tell yourself.

2. **Be resilient.** Claim you will not only survive, but thrive.

3. **Claim your truth.** Stepping into your greatness starts with the words and truth you decide to say yes to and claim as your truth. Be willing to stand in your truth.

4. **Remember you can do this.** Be open to the "how."

5. **Develop your escape plan and follow it.** Follow your plan to get from where you are

currently to where you truly want to be.... your way and on your terms.

6. **Take Action.** Aspire.... step into your greatness!

CHAPTER 3 – EVERYONE IN YOUR CIRCLE MAY NOT BE IN YOUR CORNER

If you can make it here, you can make it anywhere!

That familiar phrase refers to finding success in New York City and being able to thrive subsequently anywhere after leaving. For many of the millions of New Yorkers living in the city, trying to make it against all odds wasn't a phrase to live by, but a way of life because there was no IF. You HAD to make it there. There were no other options. There wasn't a plan B.

As a young, intrepid, twenty-something year-old New Yorker living on my own without parental support, **I worked hard to take care of myself because I didn't have anyone to fall back on.** I lived in one of the highest populated cities in the world. I enjoyed having a wide circle of friends, yet I routinely experienced profound loneliness. I always prided myself on my strength and resilience, but many times I suffered from self-doubt and sought validation from people that I admired or wanted to impress.

In my early twenties, I worked as a sales assistant for a large Fortune 500 company in Manhattan. The workplace was thriving with young professionals hungry to make their mark and scramble up the career ladder. It was a competitive, cut-throat environment.

Every man or in this case woman, for themselves. It was the workplace version of the popular television reality show, '*Survivor*'. The difference was there weren't two different tribes, only one, the 'work force'. You were faced with many mental challenges during long work hours that were fueled by an endless stream of coffee. The internet was still in its infancy and people were still using AOL, but generally email was used for the office. If you wanted to keep your finger on the pulse you had to network and that meant socializing with co-workers and colleagues. Like the show, '*Survivor*', all participants needed to have alliances. As a young professional, I was hungry, yet naive, and did not realize that most of these alliances were not based on friendship.

I met Sherrie soon after I started in the company. She was smart, funny, bubbly, and loved being the center of attention. We hit it off right away! Sherrie was unlike the others. Inside the office, everyone spoke in conspiratorial whispers, but Sherry could not or did not know *how* to whisper. You could always *hear* her before you would see her. She was loud and boisterous. Sherry was very comfortable in her own skin, but I noticed that sometimes people would try to avoid her, and would cease conversation when she came around. Then, I would think of my Mom's words, 'people don't like to be around loud women!' I spoke with a low tone all my life because she would shoot me a look if I sounded like I was 'hog-calling' or talking loudly. I hated that! This could one of the reasons I was drawn to Sherrie. She was loud, authentic, driven, and most important, didn't care what other people thought about her.

After work, we would hit some of the city's trendiest watering holes. No surprise, we would run into some of our co-workers and we would all hang out until the early morning hours. Usually around midnight, I would call a cab and head home, especially mid-week nights. Sherrie would stay out all night, go home for a nap and a shower and be fully functional by 5am.

BEEP! BEEP! BEEP! My pager would buzz and I could guarantee who it was 'beeping' me at 6:00 in the morning. In the days when a cellphone was the size and weight of a brick and there was nothing smart about it, we would use a pager. This device was the size and weight of a box of raisins. If someone called your beeper, their number would flash across its display and you would call that person back. It seems so primitive today, but in the 90s that was many of us stayed in contact with one another.

"Hey, GIRRRL! Let me teeeeeellllll you….", Sherrie's voice would boom through the phone and fill the room. She would regale me with all the office gossip that she heard from all the other co-workers after departed the night before. I would dutifully listen while I got ready for work. Then, I would rush to the subway to take the train to work to be met in the lobby by Sherrie with more office gossip. Sometimes we would run into my boss at the elevator banks. She made the boss from the *'Devil Wears Prada'* look like Mother Theresa. I'll call her Ms. G.

"GOOD MORNING, Adrian" she would say with her distinctive husky voice. Then she would glance over at Sherrie and add curtly, "morning, Sherrie."

Sherry would smile sweetly and tell her how much she loved her Gucci shoes, David Yurman bracelet, Chanel purse or something expensive that my boss was wearing. Sherrie loved designer labels! My boss would ignore her with a sniff, turn her back to her and initiate conversation with one of the other executives on the elevator or worse, she would turn her attention to me.

"Did you manage to get all the reports done and submitted on time? Have the orders gone out yet? Do we have a confirmation that Piaget is running their ad? It is a half-page ad!" she would bark at me.

Sherrie would shoot me a look of sympathy if she didn't think Ms. G was watching, but Ms. G *never* missed anything! The dragon lady would go full throttle into her tirade at that point coldly watching me squirm as I answered her rapid-fire questions.

Ms. G was a blonde powerhouse, barely standing over five feet tall, with heels and attitude. She was smart, ambitious, and driven. She took enormous pride in being self-made woman. Although she had 'suffered' through three husbands – her words – she never depended on anyone. She worked hard for everything she had and claimed that is why she demanded excellence – in everything!

"No one gives a woman a second shot if she is lucky to get a first!" she would tell me while she examined my work. I learned that if I wanted to survive the *Blonde Dynamo;* I had to keep my mouth shut, head down, and do things right the first time. She made all the sales staff jumpy and anxious. They would scamper away like rodents from the light when she entered the room because of her highly critical nature. They would leave little slips of paper on my chair that read 'how do you do it?!?' 'how do you put up with her?' 'OMG! She is the crazy!'

There were times I would find myself in the bathroom crying because of one of her scathing rebukes. It seemed that nothing I did was ever met her impossibly high standards. Sherrie would console me and advise me to go to human resources to report Ms. G for harassment, but I felt stuck so endured Ms. G's abuse because I needed a paycheck and the truth of it all, I was afraid of her.

One day, I arrived at work and received a call from a family member with some disturbing family news. It left an emotional mess. I could barely concentrate on my work and the heavy volume of calls I needed to make. To make matters worse, Ms. G's early morning meeting with her client had not gone well and she was in a terrible mood. I knew it was going to be a LONG day. Around 11am she came over to my desk and said,

"We are going to lunch today. Make sure your call list is done and you're ready in 30 minutes!" she barked, spun on her heel and briskly walked away before I had a chance to respond.

OF ALL THE DAYS?!? The cab ride to the restaurant was pleasant enough. The restaurant was beautiful with celebrities sprinkled throughout the place dining at their tables trying not to be seen, yet noticed. In New York, those of the people that want to be seen, but not called out, so do not dare approach!

Ms. G always looked right at home in those settings. Like a general inspecting her troops, barking out orders, or just allowing her presence to command respect. The waiters jumped to her attention every time she lifted one of her well-manicured, red-lacquered fingers. We were all at her command seeking to please.

She focused her steel-blue eyes on me for a moment, watching me fidget in my chair and looking at my nail-bitten hands with cuticles that looked as if wild dogs had gnarled on them. She raised an eyebrow and then asked me, "Do you think you belong here?"

"Um…I guess" I replied hesitantly.

"If you THINK you BELONG here, then you belong here," she said tapping the table with her forefinger for emphasis and without taking her piercing gaze off me.

"Do you know why I hired you?"

I was startled by that question, so I made up a quick response about my ability to get things done under pressure.

She let out a laugh that was a mix of whoop and a growl.

"No, Adrian! I hired you because you remind me of *ME*. The difference is I know when to speak up for myself and I know who my friends are!" she snapped.

She leaned toward me and asked, "Do you *really* know who your friends are?" Before I could answer she added, 'do you think you have friends at the office?'

"Name some of your friends back at work?" she commanded.

I threw out a few names, the first one I listed was Sherrie.

"You think any of them are your friends? You *really* think they are your friends? Tell me why you think this after I order our lunch." The waiter appeared like a genie that was just commanded to give three wishes.

As she gave our order to the waiter, my mind raced with so many conflicting thoughts. I never doubted my friendship with my co-workers, especially Sherrie. *What was Ms. G getting at?* But, something about way she questioned me was unsettling and I couldn't shake the feeling that I was going to be dropped in the rabbit hole.

Then came the drop.

"You are far too trusting. You would do anything to be liked. I have no idea why." She shook her head and then added, "I want you to listen very carefully to words coming from this wise, old woman."

"***Do not treat your associates like your friends. To your associates you are interchangeable with any other, but you are irreplaceable to friend.*** Don't forget that! If you were to leave the company and work at another you would never hear from the people you called your friends. Yes, even Sherrie! Speaking of that woman, she has never been your friend! She has been tearing you down since you started working with the company!"

BOOM! My ears started ringing and I couldn't get enough air into my lungs. Did she just say what I think she said? Tearing me down? What was happening?

"When she found out I needed a sales coordinator, she desperately wanted the job, but I hired YOU! She has been at the company for almost three years and I brought you in from the outside. Many people resent that and she is no exception. You think she is lively and fun, but she is also one of the most unscrupulous people I know and that is saying a lot! You think I was picking on you because I would have you re-do your work. Do you know why? The person I wanted to train you was pulled into other projects. Sherrie offered to help you learn company processes, but she would purposely forget to mention important items or tasks. She was sabotaging you. She thought it made her look good, but I saw what she was doing and I was waiting for you to catch on. If you were any other person I would have fired you, but you know what? I LIKE YOU! But, I am losing my patience!"

My mouth was hanging open as my brain tried to process the words pouring from her mouth.

She paused for a moment with a raised eyebrow and then continued, "Do you remember you called in sick a few weeks ago complaining of a migraine. Do you know who delivered the message to me? She didn't say you had a migraine. She told me an outrageous story about a drug binge and a late-night party. She actually mentioned rehab. Tsk!" Ms. G looked disgusted.

"It is no secret in the office that she a habit and…" she looked at me and I noticed her piercing gaze had softened and it was then, that the tears would no longer remain in the corners of my eyes. Why hadn't worn waterproof mascara? Damn!

She waved her hand with a dismissive gesture as if crying was no use in this conversation. "Look, I know you want to fit in around here, but just remember because people are smiling in your face it doesn't mean they have your back. Sherrie only stayed around you because she wants to take what you have earned. Tell me what kind of friend do you think she is to other people?"

I was ashamed to think that I'd overlooked a few questionable things about Sherrie, just to be friends with her. I heard she dabbled in drugs, although she had never done them in front of me, sometimes I questioned how she was able to party all night and go to work the next day. She knew all the gossip about everybody else, it only made sense that she would be gossiping about me too, but telling people lies and starting a smear campaign to get me fired!? I was incensed at this revelation, but then Ms. G dropped another bombshell.

"I suspect she told you to ask me for the key to the petty cash draw because the other assistants had access to it for expenses. I refused you the key. I could see you were hurt by that, but I think you might have told her I had given you the key because you didn't want her to know that I wouldn't give it to you."

I nodded without meeting her eyes. My ears burning from the shame of getting caught in a lie and knowing she could read me so well.

"Not even two weeks later she reported YOU to HR for STEALING petty cash. I can only assume it was one of her friends that took the money, but HR contacted me. I cleared it up by letting them know that was a false accusation because you do not have the key to petty cash like some of the other assistants do."

Ms. G spent the lunch hour teaching me a valuable lesson about friendship, being

comfortable being who you are, and stop seeking acceptance or approval from others. **The person I thought despised was the one looking out for me and the person I trusted was the one trying to bring me to ruin.** I confronted Sherrie about what I had learned. She denied everything, called me every curse word in the English language, and stopped talking to me, but talked about me to everyone that would listen. This was devastating, but it helped me to focus on building meaningful relationships in the workplace *and* in my personal life. **Ms. G. was right. I had to learn to accept myself and stop seeking the approval and acceptance of others.**

As for Ms. G, she did not stop being *the general*, but our working relationship was strengthened by mutual trust and respect. She became one of the first powerful women in my life to mentor me and help me grow into the powerful woman I am today. When she left the organization a few years later for a better opportunity, she offered me a management position at the new company she was going to, which I promptly accepted. As they say, the rest is history.

Aspire To Your Greatness!

1. Learn to accept yourself.
2. Stop seeking approval of others.
3. Do you truly know who is in your corner?

4. Remember, you are irreplaceable to a friend, and they are to you. (Associates are interchangeable…know the difference.)

5. Listen when someone cares enough to share a truth with you.

6. Be willing to rise up again, grow and step into your greatness!

CHAPTER 4 – YOU ARE MEANT TO SOAR

"Pay Attention!"

I cannot begin to tell you how many times I have heard those words growing up. My mind was always wandering to faraway places. *My favorite pastime was to gaze up into the heavens above and watch airplanes zip across the sky going to their destinations.* How I longed to be on one of them jetting off to a foreign, exotic place for a life of fun and adventure. *One day*, I would say to myself.

In my late twenties, the relentless feeling of wanderlust intensified deeply within me. I felt compelled to travel as much as possible. The more I travelled, the harder it became to return home to New York because I loved being abroad and I started to seriously contemplate leaving the United States and moving overseas. Then a catastrophic event happened in 2001 that changed my world and shaped my life.

"A plane just hit the World Trade Center" my co-worker said to me. She reported the news to me as if she was telling me there was an increase in traffic on the Henry Hudson Parkway. No reason for alarm or fear, just a topic for conversation. We both assumed it was low-flying plane that accidentally hit one of the towers, so we didn't banter about it for more than five minutes. Then –

"Oh my God!"

"Did someone say the second tower just got hit?"

"Are we under attack?"

The main hallway started to fill up with professors, academic staff, and grad students all wondering what was going on. People started to rush inside the building panicked because they heard the news of the Twin Towers being hit by planes. A small crowd formed around the front desk area where the receptionist had a small radio. We eagerly hung on to every word the announcer said with each update and then – the South tower fell.

"This can't be happening!"

"I can't get a signal on my phone! I need to call my daughter she works on Chambers Street!"

People were scrambling into offices trying to get on the office landlines to place calls to loved ones. Some stared in disbelief out of their windows looking at the dark plumes of smoke wafting from downtown. Others just cried and hugged one another for comfort and reassurance.

"The other Tower has fallen! The other one just went down!"

There were audible gasps followed by sobbing from some of the staff. Then we heard more announcements from the growing crowd.

"The City is on lockdown! It's on lockdown! O mio Dios! My husban' works in Brooklyn. How's he gonna get home now?"

"They are closing the building down. We have been ordered to go home and wait for more information"

"Wait for what? We are under attack!"

Fear. I saw fear that day on the faces of my co-workers, the graduate students, strangers on the street, *everywhere*.

September 11, 2001. A day that changed the lives of most Americans. A day that changed my life.

The days following 9/11 were a blur, but something had changed in me. I no longer felt rooted in New York. I wanted to spread my wings and soar to start a new chapter in my life.

I started to travel more and more outside of the country with the objective of moving abroad. My work colleagues used to tease me about 'living in the clouds' because I dreamt of leaving the country. They would try to dissuade me from pursing my dream by asking about my dating life and trying to fix me up with a 'nice guy' they knew.

"You are such a pretty girl, why don't you get married?"

"I just saw a nice house in my area that is for sale and the commute is not too bad."

"Have you met the new guy on the 11th floor…he's soooo cute! What are you doing this Friday?"

I had met the new guy on the 11th floor – not interested. I had considered purchasing a home and moving to the suburbs – not my passion. Marriage was something I hoped to experience someday, but it was not my childhood dream. My co-workers would not let up. They liked to push my buttons to get me riled up.

"She ain't leaving New York! She can travel where eva she wants ta go, she is comin' back 'ere!"

"I know right, Ms, NEW YORK ova there! She knows tis city like da back offa hand! She ain't going nowhere!"

Yes, I loved my city and considered myself to be a proud New Yorker, but I was feeling more and more like a world citizen. I felt at home in the beautiful Santa Teresa and Copacabana districts in Rio de Janeiro. I felt energized and invigorated every time I visited my favorite city, Barcelona. I loved the cozy, hilly, oceanside city of Lisbon that reminded me of a 14th century San Francisco, another favorite city of mine. I was enamored with vibrant energy of London and the rich history of Rome. Why couldn't I live in any of those majestic cities? **Should I let my place of birth determine my life-long residency?** I would ponder the answers to those questions trying to reassure myself that I could live the life that I wanted. **BUT**. I couldn't weed out the concerns that had been insidiously planted in by naysayers fast enough. *I was allowing the negative views of others to erode my confidence and question my judgment. I started to think like them, starting a statement positively, then adding BUT to complete the thought negatively.* Have you ever done this? Let your past determine your future? Let your dreams go because of other's fears? I would think, I am going to move to Europe next year BUT how will I support myself? I am going to resign from my job in six months BUT what if I am not ready to move overseas by then?

DIMINISH THE SIZE OF YOUR BUT

We know what we want to do, we have the capability of doing it, and herein the lies the problem with the word "BUT", it gives a way out of being accountable. That word represents our fears and doubts of failure and rejection. It can make us focus our attention on all the things that can go wrong rather than focus on the dream and having a successful outcome. I had to be careful about allowing the fears of others to influence my decisions and negatively impact my outcomes. Every thought and word I spoke is an affirmation. I decided to make a conscious effort to change my mindset by becoming more positive and using a stream of positive affirmations to keep me focused. ***If I wanted to soar, I couldn't stay with people that didn't believe in flight and had developed no wings.*** They were content staying on the ground level because it felt safe, but on the ground, you have limited range in your vision. My vision was too grand to them because their thinking was shorter-sighted, their view of the world and themselves, was myopic.

I remember hearing of a story of a man visiting a childhood friend that had moved to the country. (Author unknown) As the man and the friend were reminiscing, he noticed something very odd in the man's backyard, and pointed to his friend and asked, "what is that beautiful eagle doing with those chickens?" His friend looked around the yard to see what the man was talking about and then shrugged. "Right there!" the man nearly shouted pointing at the big, beautiful eagle. The friend gave the man a quizzical look and then answered, "oh! You mean my favorite chicken!" The man stammered, "chick..chick..chicken…what?! NO! That is an eagle and will *always* be an eagle!"

"No, THAT is my favorite chicken! I have had it since it was a few days old. It has ALWAYS been around chickens and *now* it THINKS it is a chicken, Look! It even eats corn" he said and threw a few kernels the bird's way to demonstrate his point.

The man grew so angry that he took off his hat, threw it on the ground and hurried over to grab up the bird.

He held up the bird and said, "THIS IS AN EAGLE, it does NOT belong on the ground, but in the SKY." The friend stood there shaking his head watching his friend get more agitated. The man offered to take his friend up to the mountains to show him what the bird was capable of. The friend accepted the offer and they headed up to the mountains.

The man released the bird and it immediately dove to the ground. It looked around for the other chickens. "I told you it is a chicken," said the friend reaching for the bird, but the man snatched it up again and hiked up the cliff a few feet and released the bird a second time. This time the eagle extended it wings a little bit, but fell back down to the earth with a smashing thud. "Ha! I told YOU it is a chicken" declared the friend. The man now shaking with anger grabbed the bird again. "It is NOT a chicken! It is an EAGLE!" He went up to the top of the mountain, lifted the bird high in the air and before releasing it said, **"YOU ARE AN EAGLE AND YOU MUST FLY! IT IS IN YOUR NATURE!"** If the bird did not fly this time it would mean certain death. The bird started to fall and the owner turned his back to it because he didn't want to see his favorite chicken die. At some point during the fall, the bird extended its wings and then slowly started to move them and began flying. The eagle flew higher and higher at amazing speeds until it began to soar to great heights and off into the horizon. ***"An eagle is an eagle, it's*** *its nature to SOAR!" said the man with great satisfaction.*

I remember growing up, the neighborhood kids would incite each other to do daring feats or tasks. "Go on" they would encourage, "I DARE you!" If the child being challenged was hesitant, the kids would mock him or her by making the sound of a chicken. They would tease the scared child by calling him or her *a chicken*. I felt like life was mocking me and calling me a chicken for having a chicken-like mentality. After a few years of testing my wings, by jumping 'off the cliff' through years of travel, I knew it was time to truly soar and pursue my dream of living abroad.

WHAT DOES YOUR FOREST LOOK LIKE?

In 2004, I announced my decision to move to Rome. I put a plan of action into place to move there in May 2005. I was determined to see my dream come true. My friends in Europe were thrilled by the news. A few were American expatriates and they shared first-hand experiences and tips on gaining employment, visas, housing, and getting documentation for residency. I had conducted my research, but their information was invaluable to a smooth transition and avoiding severe culture shock. I had found my tribe!

The response to my decision back in the United States was not that encouraging. Although, I was not expecting a parade with banners, balloons, and a marching band, I was prepared for the profound negativity. It was implied that I was uprooting my life on a whim. That I was trying to be European or had dubious motives.

"Why are trying to be white?"

"I thought you were solid, but this seems so flighty!"

"Why do you REALLY want to do this?"

This raised some interesting questions about those I had thought were my friends, community and tribe:

Why would people that claimed to love me try to stop me from being happy and doing something I loved? Why would they try to stop me from living my dreams? The people that I thought would support me were the biggest *Dream Killers* in my life at that time. They were like the beautiful vine that grows next to the big, strong tree in the forest. The leaves of the vine encircling the tree are green, lush, and beautiful making the tree appear even more beautiful. The vine appears to be innocuous as it enhances the beauty of the tree, but appearances can be deceptive. The vine's roots unseen to the naked eye beneath the soil have tapped into the roots of the big, strong tree slowly draining it of vital nutrients. Its big beautiful leaves soaking in all the precious rain water as the vine encircles the tree to reach the top of it to penetrate the forest canopy and rob the tree of essential sunlight. The vine that steals precious nutrients, rain, and sunlight from the big, strong tree is also encircling it slowly and strangling it to death. That is why is aptly called the *Strangler Fig*.

I had to examine the people that were around me. They appeared to have my best interest and maybe they thought they did, but they were projecting their fears unto me and those fears were encircling and strangling my dreams. Their negative energy was robbing me of being firmly rooted in the faith that was the best decision for me. The smooth talk was like those lush vines leaves that appear to enhance the beauty tree but are deceptive in nature because they only serve their own interests.

Big dreams happen with BOLD moves! I knew I had to be bold and stay strong. I began to weed out the naysayers from my life by spending less time with them and more time with strong, like-minded people. My expatriate friends overseas were cheering me on through phone calls, emails, and cards. They were like the tall and mighty trees you would find in mountains of northern California. The roots of the mighty trees cannot grow deep because of the rocky soil of the mountains. How do they withstand windstorms one may ask? The mighty trees always grow in a large **GROVE** and their roots *intertwine* and cover very large areas allowing *all* the trees to withstand a windstorm. The mighty trees are the beautiful, majestic *Sequoias*. My expatriate friends were like my *Sequoias,* helping me to withstand storms of negativity and discouragement and helping to keep me rooted in faith that my dreams would come true.

I moved to Rome, Italy in May 2005 and made my childhood dream come true! Moving overseas was one of the best decisions I have ever made, but it would not have happened if I didn't have a clear vision of what I wanted and if I wasn't willing to go after my dream. Also, I developed a plan of action that helped make my dream become a reality, next I had to reevaluate the people that I had in my 'forest' or had close to me that impacted my life and influenced my decisions for better or worse.

Aspire to Your Greatness!

1. What is/are your dream(s)?

2. Your past does not determine your future.

3. Diminish the size of your "But."

4. Expand your vision, lock onto your dream and SOAR!

5. Remove unhealthy vines.

6. You are NOT a chicken. You are an EAGLE!

7. Big Dreams Happen with BOLD Moves. Go after you dream(s)!

CHAPTER 5 – LIVE YOUR DREAM

Benvenuti Italia! Welcome to Italy! I had seen and read those words before when I visited Italy, but on May 31, 2005 when I arrived at Fiumicino Airport and saw the sign **I felt like it was a welcome sign to my new life. A new me. I was living my dreams on my terms!**

The first few days in the Eternal City, I revisited all of my favorite places; the Spanish Steps, majestic Trevi fountain, Villa Borghese, the awe-inspiring Colosseum, the Forum, and hung out in Trastevere area, while eating copious amounts of gelato. It was 'Dolce Vita', the good life, but like most good things it had to come to an end. I needed to find a job and in order to prepare for my job search, I enrolled in an intensive 120-hour training course at a school for TEFL educators. As a TEFL teacher, I learned how to create lesson plans for varying levels of language learners and tailor them for younger ages. The course helped me to become a certified teacher, but after completion in mid-July, I still lacked a job. By August, I still had not found a job because everything shuts during that month so, I dedicated that time to travel with my friends. I took the train up to Florence and met a couple of friends there. We them took the train to the Emilia-Romagna region to visit Bologna, Parma, and Ravenna. I was instantly smitten with the sleepy, university town of Parma. There appeared to be more bicycles than cars on its cobblestoned streets. Even the most discriminatory palate would find comfort in the cuisine. The Parmesans seemed to always enjoy *la passeggiata*, the evening stroll usually taken in the town square to socialize with friends and neighbors.

Later in the month, I traveled to Madrid and met up with my friends that lived there. They drove me down to the beautiful Andalusia region and introduced me to the charming village of Nerja. We strolled along the balcón de Europa, its famous promenade and get breath taking views of the coast. In the evening, we would lay on the beach, drinking Estrella Dam beer and counting shooting stars blessed by the Perseid meteor shower.

I had always loved Barcelona, but during this trip I fell in love with southern Spain. We travelled throughout the region visiting Malaga and the jet-setting town of Marbella. We visited the proud, awe-inspiring Alhambra in Granada, the great Mezquita in Cordoba, and the Torre Giralda in Seville. The rich history and culture of Spain deeply impressed me and everywhere I went I was warmly welcomed. My Spanish friends teased me mercilessly about choosing the wrong country to make my home. I started to question my decision to move to Italy because my heart was in Spain. I truly loved being in that country, but before I could be truly certain it was time for me to return back to Italy,

Upon returning to Italy, my dream truly became reality, no one would hire me legally because I did not have a *permesso de soggiorno*, the permit to stay and work in Italy. Most schools could hire teachers from the United Kingdom and avoid sponsoring native English speakers. The irony, was a demand for native American speakers because many Italians, and Spanish speakers I learned later, wanted to learn American colloquialisms so they could better understand American movies and music. I sent my curriculum vitae or resume to every English teaching school, even the questionable ones, and was denied a job once they found out I didn't have my visa. Finally, one director told me why the schools were so skittish to hire non-European Union nationals.

"It's the police. [dramatic pause]. They will give us a heavy fine if we they find anyone employed by us that does not have their documents." She sniffed in clipped English with a posh London accent. Her lips barely moved as she spoke and he face seemed frozen into place. She went on to tell me that some schools kept an American or non-EU national in the back and chased them out the back door when the police showed up but sometimes that didn't work. The police had stepped up their raids and all of the schools were feeling the sting. My mind immediately rejected what she was saying and quickly surmised she was simply racist refusing to hire me by blaming it on police raids, but I shared what she had told me with my colleagues that worked in the schools and they confirmed what the director had said. The police were raiding schools?! Of all the crimes that could be committed?

By November, I wasn't sure what my next step would be. I had not anticipated it would be that hard to find work and I was B-R-O-K-E! I was eating spaghetti every day and owed my landlord two months back rent. Going back home to New York was not an option! We plan, God laughs, so goes the Yiddish proverb. I heard laughter when I received an email requesting an interview to be a nanny for a wealthy family with four children. The laughter grew louder when I answered the email, set up the interview, and got the job! After I started working as a nanny, I received offers from professionals for one-to-one lessons to improve their English. When the kids were in school, I was meeting with executives in their offices and coffee shops giving English lessons. Yes, we plan, God laughs.

The jobs paid handsomely and every chance the family would go on holiday, I'd politely decline to accompany them giving myself an opportunity to travel on my own. My favorite destinations were London and Spain, especially Barcelona. By Spring 2006, I had become completely disenchanted with Rome. The pickpockets, filthiness of the metro and streets, graffiti, and superiority complex of its people made me yearn to live in another place. In April, I decided to move to Barcelona. I waited until the children finished school and my clients went on summer holiday. **In July 2006, I was on to my next adventure and moved to beautiful Barcelona.**

I found an apartment to share in Barcelona that was located only blocks from the beach! It felt like paradise! Every day I woke up smiling, pinching myself, hoping this dream would never end. I loved going for a run on the beach in the morning watching the sun rise.

Barcelona has a good transit system which was great for someone like me that had clients all over the city. My clients varied from Spanish students studying for their TESOL exams for entry in American universities and executives pursing an above intermediate level of English. The English teaching schools in Barcelona were willing to hire Americans, but pay them only in cash, so my business, ***Effective Communications***, was a cash-based operation.

As an American, I could legally stay in Spain for 90 days with the Schengen visa. To get around this, I would take a bus from Barcelona to the small principality of Andorra, wedged between Spain and France in the Pyrenees mountains. I would ask the bus driver to drop me off at the border control, there I would ask to have my passport rubber stamped with the Andorran official stamp and then spend the day shopping in Andorra before climbing back on a bus heading to Barcelona.

The first time I did this, it felt like a fun adventure, but after a couple of trips I got tired of *running for the border*. I wanted to live and work in Europe legally! **The desire to live legally without feeling like I was someone lurking in the shadows but a thriving member of society became so important to me that I was willing to leave a city I had grown to deeply love.**

In March 2007, I moved to Frankfurt, Germany to accept a job offer for a school that would sponsor a work permit. Frankfurt-am-Main, is known as the Manhattan of Germany. It is a culturally diverse city and many of people living there were expatriates like me. **I thought I would settle there for some time, but only days after my arrival, the rug was pulled from under me. The job offer was rescinded!** The director would not give me a clear explanation for the job denial. It felt like I was punched in the gut. **I knew I had made the wrong decision by leaving Spain, but now I had to make the best of the situation.** My one and only friend in the area, Felicita graciously let me sleep on her couch in her small studio apartment, until I could get on my feet, but I knew I was imposing on her and this only made me feel worse.

My job search was not as fruitful as I had hoped leading me to expand my search into other cities. I hoped I would find work in Berlin, and then God laughed again when a job offer came out of Munich. I would be teaching kindergarten! A few days after I had received the offer I was on a train heading southeast to Munich. I arrived at Munich

Hauptbahnof, the main train station greeted by one of the parents of the school. **He explained they were still working on the 'housing situation' so I would be a guest at their home that weekend. I was shocked! I was guaranteed housing when I accepted the job, but in a rush to offer me the job they had not secured housing for me. I lived out of my suitcases for almost two months staying in various places until the month of May!**

In May, I moved into the Au-Haidhausen area, east of the Isar river, in a flat owned by an American professor used as an office space for himself and the rest to university students. My flat mates were nice, quiet, and respectable. I enjoyed my work at the kindergarten and I had even found work with Arena Lingua, an English teaching school with a large business clientele. My clients were business executives throughout the city and soon I was in-demand as a business English teacher. This caused conflicts with my kindergarten job, making me reevaluate what type of work made me happy, but also made me question if I was happy living in Munich. **It felt wonderful to work and reside legally in Germany, but I missed Barcelona terribly. My decision to leave beautiful Spain still haunted me.**

It made me think of the story of the blind girl. She was very unhappy because she was blind. The only thing that made her happy was her boyfriend, as he was always there for her. He loved her deeply and wanted to marry her, but she would only marry him if she could see the world around her. One day, she received word that someone donated a pair of eyes. Now, she could see everything! For the first time, she was able to see her loving boyfriend. He asked her, "will you marry me?" The girl was disgusted when she looked at him and realized he was blind too! She not only turned down the marriage proposal, but she refused to see him again. The young man was devastated. He wrote his former girlfriend a letter. It read –

Just take care of my eyes, dear. (Author unknown)

This powerful illustration demonstrates how a change in our circumstances can alter our mind-set. Depending on our circumstances, we might not appreciate what we have because of lack of sight. I had encountered obstacles living in Spain and without the right perspective, I gave up the opportunity to live in a place I that I loved because I lost sight of what made me happy. I could reside legally in Spain, it just required a longer process, but one that was worth it. Unlike the blind girl, I would practice gratitude because I had the opportunity to live the life that I wanted and live in a place where that I loved. I had to take care of my eyes. I decided to return to Spain. The decision to return was one of the best decisions I ever made.... Including, meeting my future husband and soulmate.

In July 2007, I returned to Barcelona a little wiser and a lot happier. I had missed the beach, tapas, sunshine, and all of my friends. I reconnected with an old friend of mine, Harry. We could talk for hours on a range of subjects. Harry was always well-dressed, mild-mannered, and easy to talk to. He had a good friend, named Julius that he taken an interest in me. Julius confided in Harry about his feelings for me. Harry saw an opportunity to play matchmaker and jumped on the chance to bring two of his closest friends together.

Julius was a native of Cameroon. He had left home at the age of eighteen and migrated to Libya, where he lived for two years, then he migrated to Paris, France where he lived for a couple of years, before settling in Barcelona, Spain where he lived for four years when I met him. He spoke eight languages fluently. We were both determined, driven, go-getters that pursued what we wanted relentlessly. He was not the oldest male in his family, but was chosen as his father's successor, or head of the family. This responsibility gave him a high level of respect and accountability within his family. I loved how much he loved his family. Also, we both wanted a family of our own. Our love for our faith, family, and ultimately, each grew stronger and deeper with each passing day. On May 17, 2008, Julius prepared a beautiful, candlelight dinner for me and our closest friends. It was in this beautiful setting he proposed and I said "YES" to the cheers and celebrations of our closest friends

We got married on September 27. We had a small, intimate reception for close family and friends held at the Marina. That evening we had a lively reception for 300 guests at a reception hall near Montjuic. Our honeymoon was on the beautiful island of Menorca, one of the Balearic Islands off the coast of Spain.

Following my heart and returning to Spain, not only led me to a place I love…but also to the love of my life. Always listen to your heart and follow your dream.

Aspire To Your Greatness!

1. What is your dream?
2. Follow it.
3. Persevere when challenges arise. Know that you will find a way.
4. When you hit a road block, get to the root of the problem.
5. Be willing to change plans as your dream/mission/purpose adjust…be willing to fine tune.
6. Check your perspective and be willing to truly go after your heart's desire (even if it takes a while).

CHAPTER 6 – PROTECTING MY PRIDE

In 2008, Europe was in the grip of an economic recession that severely impacted countries in the southern part of the continent including Spain, Italy, and Greece. The unemployment rate in Spain reached record highs affecting citizens and expatriates alike. One month after being married, my husband was laid off from his job and two weeks later, a major client of mine decided to end their contract and close their business. Then, another exclusive client notified me they would not renew their contract the following year.

Our finances were diminishing at an alarming rate and jobs were scarce. When I proposed, moving to my home country, the United States which had more opportunities for us, my husband balked! He refused to entertain the thought of leaving Spain, a country he had grown to love as much his home country, Cameroon. Armed with determination, stubborn pride, and his curriculum vitae [resume] in hand, he scoured the city looking for any construction company that would hire him. Unfortunately, the construction industry in Spain was the hardest hit by the recession. We became so desperate that we opened up our three-bedroom flat for occupants to rent so we could us afford our monthly rent.

Finally, after several months of trying everything possible to better our situation, my husband reluctantly agreed to relocate to the United States. Thus, we began the daunting process of obtaining his visa to legally make the move. He proactively posted his resume to American job boards. During this time, he signed up for a regionally-funded six-month construction course that would help him learn in-demand construction skills. He was determined to complete the course before moving to America, but in hindsight I think he was trying to buy time in hopes a job would materialize before he finished the program and this would enable him to stay in Barcelona. *He really did not want to leave his beloved Spain!* The job did not materialize in Barcelona or any other Spanish city, but he received a job offer in Boulder, yes a city in the state of Colorado in the good ole' United States of America.

We arrived in Boulder Colorado in August 2009 with barely more than the determination to get on our feet and the dream to own our own home. Soon after arriving, I noticed a sharp pain in my left hip. I thought I had pulled something running along the beautiful nature trail, but the pain got increasingly worse to the point I would roll on the floor just to get relief. The pain was unbearable at night. It was agony! I didn't have insurance and was afraid of what an emergency room visit would cost. Also, I had just started a sales job for a local publication and the fear of losing my job or income was another cause of my sleeplessness.

My husband was experiencing culture shock living in the western United States. He loved the beauty of Colorado because he loves the outdoors, but felt out of place living in an area that he considered yuppie-homogeneous and elitist and he missed his beloved Spain. His moods were becoming increasingly erratic and melancholy. Also, he was working fourteen hours days six days a week. He was physically exhausted, emotionally drained, and spiritually depleted. We were married less than a year, but we were becoming strangers. I could not seek solace from him and that only heightened my despair.

In October, my limping was more noticeable than the deep, dark circles under my eyes which were perpetually teary and downcast. I went to the Urgent Care thinking it would be a quick visit with an X-ray to determine which muscle had torn, it felt shredded, and get a diagnosis to fix the problem. Voila! The doctor wanted to take an x-ray, but the protocol for safety reasons is to have the female patient take a pregnancy test, even if she does not think she is pregnant. When I was handed a pregnancy test I laughed out loud! While waiting to have my x-ray conducted, one of the doctors came to the area I was at with a big smile and asked, "Which news would like to hear first? Good or Bad?" I said I preferred to hear the bad news and responded, "you can't have an X-ray BUT the good news is…you're PREGNANT!" I held his gaze for twenty to thirty seconds that felt like an eternity and then my eyes that were always weepy from the chronic pain released a torrent of tears. All the fears I was holding on to washed down my face with each teardrop. I was referred to a local clinic that worked with women like me, low-income with no insurance and sent on my way. At the clinic, upon my first examination I was told that I must be carrying twins or further along in my pregnancy than I thought. I was referred to a doctor with high-risk clients like me. She performed an ultrasound and found massive fibroids! She then told me that due to my complications my baby would not live. She could prescribe potent pain medications, but the baby would develop a fetal addiction and I could develop an addiction as well. I started to cry, but received no sympathy or encouragement, only the cold stare of a doctor who appeared to be prejudging me for being a low-income, woman of color. I left the clinic thinking my situation could not get any worse, but then I was delivered another blow the following day.

The publisher of the magazine called me into her office and without a hint of emotion in her voice mechanically said she was letting me go because I was not the right fit for the job. She knew I was pregnant and needed the job! I couldn't believe it. I had tried to keep my pregnancy a secret from my co-workers, but they saw the limp in my gait caused by the pain in my left hip. The frequent bathroom breaks, spells of nausea bravely fought off with quick nibbles of crackers and sips of ginger tea. Fatigue enveloped me like a heavy cloak weighing me down physically, but also mentally, I was in a fog. It was no secret and even worse, at that moment, I was no longer an employee of the publication. My right hand reached out for the check she was holding out to me and with resignation my left hand reached under the chair for my purse and keys to a delipidated car that was one running on spit, a shoelace, and a prayer. My legs felt so heavy getting up out of that chair, but they managed to get me to my car before giving out. I sat in the driver's seat trying to catch my breath.

Breathe. Ok, Breathe. Girl, it will be okay. I said to myself as beads of sweat rolled down my temples. The heat of the car was suffocating, but I didn't want to roll down the windows because I was afraid they would get stuck like they sometimes did.

Girl, this is too big for you and when something is bigger than you. Pray. I earnestly prayed in that metal hotbox of a car for almost twenty minutes. As I prayed I felt as if I was placing a heavy burden on stronger shoulders than I possessed. My faith was reaffirmed and I knew right then my baby was going to be okay.

I sought out a second opinion, this time I was referred to a specialist, that had many years of experience with high-risk pregnancies and women suffering with uterine fibroids. He and his staff, especially his head nurse, were so friendly and immediately put me at ease. We had a lively, informative discussion on a range of topics. My eyes were drawn to the endless number of happy babies and parents that blanketed his walls. He smiled and said he had delivered all of them and to my surprise started pointing to one picture after another and recounting their names. What a difference from the other doctor!

After my examination, he told me that he could help me. I was delighted.

"As you know, Ms. Chofor you are suffering from red degeneration and the biggest concern is the fibroid located just above the birth canal. We will also keep a close eye on fibroid growing on your right side. Because of your condition we want to make sure you do not go into pre-term labor so we'll take the baby at twenty weeks..." he said before I cut him off.

"What! Twenty weeks?"

"Yes, we will help you manage the pain while monitoring you and the baby. Of course, you will be on bed rest from now until we perform the caesarean section when the fetus is twenty weeks. Ms. Chofor, be assured this hospital has a state-of-the-art neo-natal unit" and then points to various pictures on the wall, "where some of these precious ones were born. You are in good hands!"

I don't recall what I said to him after, but I remember his head nurse told me that I was making a mistake (tsk!) not seeing him anymore because he was in-demand as one of the top obstetricians in Denver for high-risk mothers. I waited for her to finish writing down the referral information and told her he wanted to take my baby at only twenty weeks.

Her chin lowered a bit and she locked eyes with me and said, "with your condition it would be a miracle *if* your baby makes it to twenty weeks," then after a slight pause adds with a smile, "but he is known to be a miracle worker! You'll be back. I hope we can take you." The sweet, reassuring voice that spoke to me earlier had quickly become the sound of patronizingly saccharine-laced negativity.

The next day, I called the referral at the University of Colorado Hospital, and the voice that answered the phone sounded just like the head nurse at the office I left. Oh great! The voice on line said they were expecting my call and they would like to see me as soon as possible. "When?", was my immediate response. "Can you come in this afternoon?" Ack! All I could think of at that moment was sitting in heavy traffic, in excruciating pain, writing about in my seat. The mere thought almost prompted me to respond that I wouldn't make it to the office, but I changed my mind when I realized that I had very little pain medication left and if I could not regulate the pain that meant another overnight stay in the hospital, no thank you!

As I drove to the hospital in Aurora from the Boulder area where I lived, I kept thinking of how exhausted

I was of the whole ordeal. The excruciating pain, perpetual nausea, and debilitating fatigue made life unbearable. I didn't have any close friends in the area to lean on for moral support. I was physically, emotionally, mentally drained, feeling like a weak mouse with no support and no voice.

A shift took place and I realized I had given the burden over to God and now needed to start thinking differently. **I had to be strong and courageous, like a lion to ready to battle for survival. Not only my survival, but literally for the survival of my baby.** A lion's family is called a pride. My baby, my little pride that was growing inside me was not weak, it needed to be strong and protected. **I had to protect my pride!**

This made me think of my father. Growing up he was my hero, king of the jungle, a lion to me. His family was his pride. We grew up in New York, but every summer and winter break, my parents would take their 'pride' down to Florida to visit her family in Florida. They planned to travel down to Florida in December 1979, but my mother had a work conflict, and bought a plane ticket with the intention of meeting us in the southern state a few days after our scheduled arrival. Our scheduled arrival. My father decided to drive to Florida alone with his five children. Alone. Twenty-hours non-stop from New York City to Florida, at night, with only coffee and determination to fuel him. He packed up his 'pride' and started out on his journey. The state lines went by in a blur as we passed through one state after another traveling south on Interstate 95.

He was driving in northern Georgia when the heavy weight of a long work week, the peaceful snoring of his 'pride' in the back seat, and the dark, cold stillness of the night lowered his eyelids long enough to take his focus off the road. The car without a driver drifted towards the edge of the road at the speed of sixty-plus miles an hour, hit the guard rail, and flipped down the embankment. We were violently awoken to being thrown around the car like items in a clothes dryer. When the car stopped somersaulting, resting on its roof at the bottom of a ravine, leaving us tangling from our seats we cried in shock and terror. Our lion, my father, leaped into action and climbed out of open driver's side window. He called out in the darkness for his 'pride' to respond as he blindly reached into the car throwing irrelevant items out as he grabbed the flailing bodies of his screaming children.

One by one he pulled us out of the car to safety. Wait! Where was his oldest son? He had dutifully helped his siblings out, but was trapped in the car! My father found a tire iron near the car, that had been thrown from the car during the tumbling down the embankment, and forcibly shattered the back window on the passenger side to pull the last of his 'pride' to safety. The faint sounds of emergency units pierced the stillness of the night which both frightened, but calmed us as recovered from the shock. He moved us away from the car, as if he knew instinctively it was dangerous to be too close to it.

Then, it exploded. It's not like in the movies which looks manufactured and surreal. What I remembered most from the explosion was the sound of it because the boom shook the ground and my young mind momentarily felt an even greater loss of control as I was thrown to the ground. All before the emergency vehicles had arrived. He knew what he needed to do and chose to do it. He rescued his pride and got us to safety. The emergency personnel then arrived to put out the fire and usher us to safety. It was comforting to see the fire engines, police, and paramedics, but nothing compared to the security of seeing our father and Lion, protecting his 'pride'.

When I pulled into the parking lot of the University of Colorado for my appointment I was now a woman with purpose and resolve to do whatever necessary to protect my baby! I was no longer a weak mouse. I was a strong, confident lioness determined to protect her pride. The physicians and staff of the hospital gave me top-of-the-line care as we all eagerly anticipated the arrival of 'the miracle baby,' as my baby had come to be known after I related my previous hospital experience to them. My pride grew bigger and stronger with every passing day! Twenty weeks passed…then Twenty-four followed…later Thirty-two and finally, when I reached my Thirty-seven week which is considered full-term, the Miracle baby made his debut on May 5, 2010!

I believe in miracles, but even more so in protecting the ones that you love.

Aspire to Your Greatness!

1. When things become too hard and heavy…remember you are not alone. Stop, pause, and pray. Give your burden to God.

2. Remember your faith, and reaffirm that it will all be okay.

3. Change your attitude from fear and powerlessness to strong and powerful. Choose your attitude with care.

4. Remember who you truly are, the truth that you know and choose what truly matters to you.

5. Protect your pride. Protect those you love.

CHAPTER 7 – STEPPING STONES

In 1999, when the world was preparing for a 'techno-apocalypse' because of computer programming glitches stemming from the Year 2000 problem, better known as Y2K, I was dealing with other issues; my family. **The relationship I had with my mother had deteriorated to a point it became so chilled that the frosty temperatures could freeze a side of beef. She completely cut off all contact with me.** If I wanted to speak with my father, the rule was to call him while he was in his office, never at home. The year before when I went to Texas to visit him, she told him and his friends that there would be a bloodbath if I stepped foot in *her* house. My mother was close with my older sister, and was helping her to raise her children by financially supporting her. My father resented their relationship. He considered her a source of friction between my mother and himself and forbade my mother having anything to do with her. My mother retaliated by telling him that I could not enter their home as well because it was not fair that I could visit but my sister did not have the same privilege. It was the most ridiculous thing I had ever heard! I was not being supported financially by either of them! Why was I caught in the middle? I knew she was being spiteful, so I purchased tickets to travel to visit my father. She refused to see me! Also, my father feared she would do something irrational and would not let me stay at their house. I was livid! A Cold War started in the hot, humid Texas heat that August that lasted for almost two, long years.

The world did not experience a digital collapse in the year 2000, but something truly amazing happened to me. After repeated urgings from my younger brother, I joined my family, including my mother for a vacation in Orlando, Florida. She was not excited that I had made the trip from New York to steal away her sunshine and rain on the Mom-Is-In-Control parade. My older brothers were also anxious about my arrival keeping their flip phones handy in case they needed to dial 911.

My older brother forewarned me that Mom did not like the idea of having me around. He shared with me:

"Look, Adrian, it's good to see you, but we don't want any problems"

"Huh, I caused a problem? I don't think I was the one that said there will be a blood bath if I see her!"

"Yea, I know, that was messed up! But, look, sis. Don't get her started okay. You know how she is.'

Yes, I knew how she was and quite frankly, *I didn't care anymore and I refused to be intimidated by her* and anyone else for that matter.

"You know I never start with her. She's so …" my voice trails off and I feel a lump begin to develop in my throat. Why is this always my fault? I haven't done anything? Wait! **I. Have. Not. Done. Anything. Wrong.** I quickly recovered to finish what I was going to say. "She does not like me. I don't know why. Do you know why?"

He shrugs, but before he can say anything, I say, "no one knows why! I am tired of her hating me and I don't know why! But, I came here because I want to see the rest of you guys and enjoy hanging with you guys at Disney World and Universal Studios!" Saying those words made smile because **I was happy to be with my family, I loved all my brothers, rarely having the opportunity to see all four them at the same time and I was obsessed with roller coasters.** I could see my brother's posture slightly, but his face still held a worried expression.

The day passed quickly and before we all knew it, our time to depart had sneaked up on us. I thanked my younger brother for encouraging me to come and spend time with the family. He then challenged me to say that to my mother's face. I hesitated because I feared the rejection or the cold shoulder, but I thought how her cool façade had worn away over the course of the vacation and she appeared to have been, dare I say…. *kind* in her interactions toward me. I accepted the challenge! I approached her with outstretched arms, embracing her body rigid from tension, and told her how happy I was to see and spend time with her. I knew this would unnerve her! She recoils from physical touch or anyone in her personal space. **She stepped away quickly from my**

embrace and the shock, but her facial expression had softened. In that moment, I saw something I had not seen in years…. *hope.* **My brothers saw it too! What we thought was irreparable could be fixed.** In that moment, I experienced a lightness I had never felt before in her presence.

When I returned to New York from my trip my colleagues teased me about my physical appearance and new attitude.

"Where did you go? *You look great girl!*"

"You are *glowing!* Tell me your *secret!*"

"What his name? Who is making you so *happy?*"

"Look at you! *Always smiling!*"

What struck me as odd was thinking about all the places I had traveled before, some exotic, and had never heard such compliments upon my return. It is always nice to hear kind words from others, but I knew there was something deeper there that I needed to delve into to find satisfying answers. **Shortly after my return, I made it a habit to call my mother every week and to keep it spontaneous, the dates were never scheduled. Our conversations usually revolved the one thing we have a passion for; our love of travel.** She was a seasoned globetrotter, with years of solo and group travel experience, and owner of a thriving travel business. We aside differences and focused on the hottest deals to grab, hottest spots to avoid, hottest beaches to enjoy.

In those conversations, I learned so much about her and how she came to develop a love for travel and her own childhood. She was born in the summer-resort, segregated town of Panama City, Florida and spent her childhood in the red-clay hills of Birmingham, Alabama, one of the most segregated cities in the South and in the forefront of the Civil Rights Movement. She and her siblings had grown up dirt poor and shared stories of being so hungry they would make sandwiches from the clay. Her experiences growing up black, female, and poor in a heavily segregated South where lynching was common place and fear and oppression overshadowed the move of every person of color, made her want to escape and see other parts of the world.

As children, we both looked at travel as a way to escape our current reality. *My aha moment!* **What a revelation and one that helped me to understand her better and see her in a different light.** Also, I noticed that when our conversations focused on future travel plans rather than past painful occurrences, we had enjoyable conversations that were upbuilding and fun. **I wanted to build a relationship with her and I knew that meant letting go of the past hurt and embracing the possibilities of establishing a mutually, loving sustainable relationship.** It was not easy the first few months, because we were both side stepping painful memories as if we were crossing a minefield.

Occasionally, we would hit rough patches, but I would put my pride aside and focus on the desired outcome, not to be right or hear an apology for past wrongs, but to build a relationship.

I was happy, relaxed, and smiling more often. My usual cynicism and sarcastic jokes toward others and life in general, had toned down to a more pleasant outlook. My sharp edges had been buffered but, by what? As I questioned what had caused the shift, I started experiencing a recurring dream.

In the dream, I could see a young, confident woman in a distance standing in a field, basking in sunlight, radiating happiness as she faced the sun with a beautiful smile on her face. It was the smile of a soul that was at peace recalling fond memories of yesteryears. She looked like me but I was not her. I wanted to be just like her, or a better me, but to reach her I would need to cross a treacherous ravine.

The ravine had large, jagged rocks and sharp, impenetrable, boulders blocking my way to where the young, happy, confident woman basked in sunshine. They had been placed there a long time ago and only seemed to become more impassable with time. I cursed my misfortune and in disgust would throw rocks and other objects at the rocks. As my frustration magnified, unbeknownst to me, so did my resentment and bitterness. Why couldn't I just be happy? Why couldn't I be happy like her?

The ravine was a dry riverbed, but years earlier I had dammed up the water upstream to conserve my resources, only allowing a trickle of water to escape which barely sustained me. My younger self reasoned; Why should I waste my precious water on the sharp, hazardous rocks anyway?

In my dream, the days quickly turned into weeks, weeks turned into months, and months turned into years of waiting, hoping, and yearning to cross the ravine to become a better, happier me. I could see the young, confident, was still smiling and had not aged, yet I was aging rapidly. My skin was dull, my hair dry and brittle, and I rarely smiled or showed emotion. I took pride in water conservation efforts as I surveyed my supply of water, but became depressed when considering the ravine of perilous. What should I do? What would you do? At this point, I would usually awaken with the same question; **why am I having this dream every night?**

I began to analyze the dream and this is what I came up with: the sharp, jagged rocks and heavy boulders symbolized the many obstacles in my life. The past hurts, disappointments, and pain I had endured especially from childhood. As I grew older, the rocks only appeared to be sharper and the boulder bigger rather diminished in texture and size. In frustration, I would gather more rocks and throw them at the boulders and sharp rocks hoping to break them down. I had grown so accustomed to being blocked by rocks and other obstacles, I would gather more problems or obstacles to keep me from my happiness, but foolishly thinking the additional drama was helping me get past my problems.

I realized the water played a very big part in crossing the ravine. How so? I would need to undam the water upstream. Not just a trickle, but let the water rush through the ravine over the sharp rocks and boulders. **Over time the rushing water will do something truly amazing, it will smooth the rough, jagged edges of the rocks and the boulders. It would polish the perilous rocks into stepping stones! What were once too dangerous to step on would now serve as support as I crossed the ravine. By crossing, I would have left behind the bitterness and resentment and become the happy, confident woman I had always wanted to be.**

The water in the dream symbolized forgiveness and as long as I dammed it up without using it for its intended purpose, it could work its magic by smoothing the rocks of pain, disappointment, and hurt. **I needed to stop living in the past and allowing past disappointments to continue to hurt me. By allowing myself to forgive and do so freely, without expecting anything in return was one of the most liberating things I have ever done!**

By forgiving her, I did not minimize or condone what had happened in my childhood, but I allowed myself the gift of moving past it. I did not wait for her to make the first move nor did I want her to change. It makes me think of Harriet Lerner, Ph.D.'s highly acclaimed book, and one that I read countlessly, the *Dance of Anger*. She writes that if you think of your relationship as a dance, when one person changes their steps, the dance inevitable changes. Like water with its life-saving nutrients, the waters of forgiveness possess life-saving and enriching healing powers transforming my impenetrable pain and deep hurt to building blocks and stepping stones of support, empowerment and strength.

Forgiveness empowered me to take the steps to build a relationship with my mother and become a more confident, happier woman. I could not change my mother, but I could change how my actions and how I reacted to hers.

Aspire to Your Greatness!

1. Be willing to make the first move.
2. Build a bridge of connection.
3. Be willing to let go of past hurts.
4. Release your pride and desire to "be right" and/or hear an apology.
5. Focus on the desired outcome.
6. Let the water of forgiveness flow.

7. Change your steps in the dance and find your stepping stones.

CHAPTER 8 – ON THE JOURNEY TO THE BETTER

My life's journey has been one of many triumphs and challenges. I overcame numerous obstacles and have enjoyed many successes.

In September 2016, I decided to listen to my inner wisdom and dream and embarked on a challenging career. I started the Aspire 2 Inspire Transformational Practice. One of the reasons I decided to become an empowerment leader was my desire to help those that needed help overcoming challenges and self-doubts, like someone helped me. Rather than just focusing on helping clients with goal-setting and working to achieve their goals, as an empowerment leader I help to shift mind-set. When someone reaches a higher level of consciousness, elevating their emotional state, their perspective will change as well because they realize they have more options, and the power to become their best selves! To aspire to their greatness!

Another area of focus is helping people that desire to move abroad to do so and have a successful transition. When I moved overseas, as a woman of color, I did not have any guidance in the process. I researched the visa processes, international banking, language barriers, and housing, but I did not have coaching on cultural integration, identity management, career transitioning, and individual adaptation. It would have been so valuable to me have had someone walk beside me to guide and help me through the process. So, now I am honored to be able to support others in all of these things. There are many hopeful expatriates seeking assistance and first-hand knowledge from an expert on how to have a successful transition. There is a need in another area as well, and that is the challenges faced by repatriates, or expatriates returning home. Repatriates find social readjustment back home to be challenging as the relationship dynamics within their social circles might have shifted when they lived abroad. Their network of family and friends might not understand the challenges of reverse culture shock or devalue their international experience.

When I think about my life and the legacy I will leave behind, I think of the story of the *'Flat Tire'*.

THE FLAT TIRE (This story is shared in "The Chain of Love" is a song written by <u>Rory Lee Feek</u> and <u>Jonnie Barnett</u>, and recorded by American country music singer <u>Clay Walker</u>.)

A man was driving his car, when he saw a woman, stranded on the side of the road. He could see that she needed help. So, he stopped his car, an old Honda near her shiny, Mercedes Benz and got out to help her.

As he approached her, he smiled, but the woman stood there wringing her hands with worry, as nobody had stopped for hours to help her, now she was alone with a strange man. She looked at the man and thought he did not appear to be someone she could safely be with due to his poor, shabby appearance. The man could sense how frightened the woman was, so he made eye contact and spoke softly, "I'm here to help you, so, you don't have to worry," he then added, "my name is Joe Anderson."

He took a look at her car, noticed the flat tire, and without hesitation changed the tire of the luxury vehicle. His hands ached and he got his clothes dirty in the process, but he did not seem to mind. When the job was completed, the woman asked him how much she owed him for his help. Joe smiled. He responded, **"if you really want to pay me back, the next time you see someone, who needs help, give that person the needed assistance and think of me."**

The woman thanked him many times before climbing into her luxury car and driving away leaving Joe standing by the side of the road. As she traveled towards her destination she decided to stop at a café for something to eat. The small café had seen better days and required renovations, but the woman was so hungry she stopped anyway, and proceeded inside the dingy café.

There she saw a waitress, nearly eight months pregnant, wiping perspiration off her brow. Despite her swollen ankles and aching feet, the waitress wore a sweet, friendly smile. The waitress approached the woman and inquired of her day. She did not once complain about the discomfort of working in her condition. The lady wondered how someone who has so little could be so kind and giving to a stranger. Then she remembered Joe.

The woman finished her meal and paid it with a hundred-dollar bill. The waitress went to get change for the bill, but when returned to the table, the lady had already gone. However, she left a note on the table that read:

You don't owe me anything. Somebody once helped me, just like now, I'm helping you. If you really want to pay me back, do not let this chain of love end with you.

The waitress found four more one hundred-dollar bills under the napkin.

That night the waitress went home earlier than usual. She was thinking about the lady and the money she left. She wondered, how the lady could know how much she and her husband needed it? Especially now. The baby was due to soon arrive. She knew, her husband worried about not being adequately prepared for the arrival of the new baby, so she was excited to share the good news with him. She found him already asleep from what appeared to have had been a long, hard day. She leaned over, kissed his forehead, and whispered, "now everything will be alright."

She leaned in again, pressing her face next to his said ever so softly, "I love you, Joe Anderson".

My legacy, I want to be that we can each overcome challenges, face our fears, and aspire to our greatness! In doing so, we lift up others; creating a continuous legacy of helping ourselves and others aspire and stand in their greatness.....I hope as we celebrate our greatness. I hope my story as a woman that has overcame insurmountable challenges, faced her fears, learned to love herself and empowers others so they can conquer their fears and give back to others resulting in a continuous loop of helping and service. That the sharing of my story helps to create this legacy in action, word and deed.

I am a servant-leader, my primary focus is on the growth and well-being of the people and communities to which I serve. A servant-leader empowers others to optimal development and deliver their best performance. Like Joe Anderson, I ask that the next time you see someone, who needs help, give the person the needed assistance.

I believe in 'paying it forward' and influencing others to do the same. We all have gifts and talents, but it is what we do with them that will enrich our lives and the lives of others.

Learning the Ropes

On my journey, I have helped many to learn and develop new skills as I continue to learn as well. As an entrepreneur, I had to learn to have an entrepreneurial mind-set and acquire skills that will help me build a thriving coaching practice, be a sought-after speaker, and best-selling author. As the African proverb – **if you want to go fast, go alone. If you want to go far, go together.** If you plan to travel to a place you have never been, especially with treacherous terrain, it would be wise to use a trusted advisor to guide you on your trek, even if you are an experience traveler. If you don't believe me, just ask any mountain climber about to scale Mount Everest. They wisely seek out a Sherpa familiar with the dangerous terrain, unpredictable weather patterns, and innumerable pitfalls of scaling one of the most hazardous places on earth, that has claimed many lives. When you are about to embark on a lifechanging course, it would be wise to have a trusted advisor or mentor help you to navigate the 'unpredictable' course ahead of you. Have you heard of the expression 'learning the ropes'? The term originated many centuries ago, when ships had sails that were raised, lowered, and positioned by mean of large, thick, heavy ropes. In safe harbors, new recruits would prove their seaworthiness by learning how to identify the various ropes and their functions. Also, they had to learn how to tie knots. You had to learn the ropes before you could join crew and go out to sea.

As a woman of color that grew up in New York City, when I think of ropes, the first thing to come to mind is jumping rope, more specifically the game 'Double Dutch'. The game originated by Dutch colonists in the 1600s, in New York City when it was called New Amsterdam. This jump rope game required a long rope to be turned by two people, called enders, would turn the rope in opposite directions. The rope jumper would have to jump over two ropes rather than one. When performed correctly, the jumper(s), enders, and rope seemed to become one fluid movement. It required strength, skill, coordination. It required all to be fully cooperative to remain in continuous synch to keep the game going. They played by so many African American girls in the New York City area and other urban populations conjures up childhood memories of sisterhood and community. No one can play the game alone and no one became a skilled jumper or ender alone without guidance from another skilled jumper or ender. Your sisters, cousins, and girlfriends cheered you on! They shared tips and tricks to help you become more agile and skilled at the game. Your mother, aunts, older women in the neighborhood would look at you with nostalgia as they cheered you on to jump faster and longer. Later, they would recount their stories of Double Dutch jumping before 'bad knees' and 'bad hips' would no longer let them partake in the game. **'Learning the ropes' helped us to rely on teamwork, trust, coordination, but on a deeper level it helped us to develop a sisterhood and sense of community.** *One for all and all for one.*

Throughout our lives we will find ourselves in situations where we have to learn the ropes. As I continue on my journey, I have learned that I have to be comfortable being uncomfortable as I grow into the woman I am supposed to be. I have been called to be of service and help like Joe Anderson, with love and unselfishness.

What are you called to be? What "ropes" are you learning to become all that you are called to be? How can you cheer another on?

Aspire to Your Greatness!

1. Be actively on the look out to lift another up without expectation of something in return.

2. Receive what you are given. Be willing to accept gifts and then pay it forward as you heart is led.

3. Be willing to learn the ropes.

4. Be willing to cheer another on.

5. Embrace your calling and lean into your greatness!

CHAPTER 9 – PLAN FOR GREATNESS!

Have you ever been driving in a car and the person riding with you is giving you directions but they are lost or taking you somewhere you were not intending to go? Perhaps you are heading in your intended direction, but the person next to you and the other passengers are creating such a fuss, that you must pull over the vehicle and sort out the situation. We know that pulling over will delay our arrival at the intended destination, but the passengers in the vehicle are not cooperating. The situation can become so bad, that you have no other recourse but turn the car around and back to the starting point. These scenarios would cause us much frustration, especially when we were determined to arrive at our destination and had to deviate from that course.

Think about your life. Have you given up the driver's seat to people that are taking you off course and misdirecting you. Do you have a plan, map, or strategy to get to your destination, but feel that you don't have the support you need to get there?

After reading about my journey, I think you know that we can overcome the obstacles we face and live fulfilling lives. Should you ever have a moment where you aren't sure where you are going? Or the best way to reach your destination? Or perhaps need encouragement to get back to your center, truth, and on track? I have developed a model that helped me and I believe will help you too. It will help you take back your power and get back on track with your goals, purpose and aspirations. Because you can plan for your greatness.

It is called the V.A.P.A.R. model.

(V) VISUALIZATION

What does your IDEAL LIFE look like? Take a moment <pause> do you see it? What are you doing? How do you feel? Do you see it?

Helen Keller said the "the one thing worse than being blind is having no sight!"

What makes this quote so interesting is that the person that said it was blind and deaf. What could she possibly mean? Sight is the function of the eyes that allows us to see. Helen did not have this function, but she thought it would be worse to be without vision, why? What is vision? It is the function of the mind's eye, the proactive portion of the imagination. This function helps us to create and develop ideas. Still not sold on the importance of having vision? Consider this, you are looking for employment and a recruiter sends you to interview at an organization. During the interview you ask about the company's mission statement and vision. The interviewer gives you a puzzled look and asks why you are interested? How would you respond? Would you not want press for answer, especially if you are looking for a company with a good reputation that you remain and grow with for many years? You would be interested in learning more about the mission statement to find out the company's present state and purpose. It would let you know what it does, who it serves and how it does it. The vision statement lays out the ultimate goal. What the company wants to accomplish and the direction it plans to take to get there. It is the inspiration of what will be done. Its focus is on the future.

If our only focus is to get through the day, then that will become our mission, but without a clear vision we are just surviving. We are not living. Take this opportunity to think of about what you want to achieve and accomplish. What is your vision for each area in the next three months? Six months? One year? Five years? How much do you think you can accomplish?

Be very clear about what you want. There can be no room for doubt or uncertainty.

For example, there was a boxer that proclaimed himself to be 'The Greatest'! His peers and fans said he was not only the greatest boxer, but the greatest athlete! Yes, I am referring to none other than the incomparable Muhammed Ali. But, when do you think he started to think of himself as great? Do you think when he was the pinnacle of his career or before? If you answered before he reached the top, then you are right! Ever since he was as small child growing up in St. Louis, he considered himself to be great. It helped him to be remained determined to be his best, even when he faced extreme tests.

He was a believer in the POWER of VISUALIZATION and also the power of words which leads me too...

AFFIRMATIONS

All of our self-talk, our internal dialogue, is a stream of affirmations. Positive affirmations are consciously choosing to think thoughts that will create positive outcomes. A study published in Social Cognitive and Affective Neuroscience, was able to capture the effect of affirmations using an MRI.

(*Social Cognitive and Affective Neuroscience*, Volume 11, Issue 4, 1 April 2016, Pages 621– 629, https://doi.org/10.1093/scan/nsv136)

Participants who gave positive self-affirmations showed increased activity in various parts of the prefrontal cortex and other areas of the brain. One of the effects is that they lead less sedentary lives and had an improved outlook on their future.

Write your Affirmations

-Start your affirmation with "I" or "My"

-Think of one negative thought you have about yourself and counteract that by writing it as a positive statement

-Keep the affirmations short and in the present tense

Muhammed Ali and many other successful people living today know that POSITIVE AFFIRMATIONS are vital to staying motivated! When we change our thoughts, we change our beliefs. When we change our beliefs, we change our behaviors. When we change our behaviors, we change our lives.

(P) PLAN

"Plan the work and Work your Plan!"

You have a vision and drive from your positive affirmations to get you where you want to go. Now you need the map! This is a plan of action of specific, measurable, attainable, relevant, time-bound goals (SMART) that will use to make your vision a REALITY! Your plan will detail the tasks or actions that need to occur or behavioral changes that need to be made. The plan will outline when the actions or tasks needed to be completed. It will also help you see what and how much in resources will be needed. How will an action plan help you long-term? Here is a list of few ways:

-It will help you track your progress

-Help identify newly emerging opportunities

-Help to save time, energy, and resources

-Keep you accountable

All successful people know that a good plan requires support and other resources from the community around us. We may have heard of the expression: "Show me your friends and I will show you who you are." Let's think about your association.

ASSOCIATION

Most people appreciate of the value of gold. So, if we were to describe a friend as being 'like gold' or 'golden', it would be a compliment of the value you place on the friendship. As the saying goes, 'Together we grow old. Our friendship is like gold'. That type of friendship has a foundation of trust and loyalty which does not weaken with time, distance, or life changes. Most people look for friendships like that and many would like to think they have them, but under closer examination they might find out they have arsenopyrite, also known as fool's gold. This mineral looks like gold, even has small traces of gold in it, but do not be fooled, it is not gold. It is an arsenic iron sulfide and when heated or cooled it releases elemental sulfur that gives off toxic fumes. The mineral is highly toxic!

In our lives, when we are seeking to make changes that would better our lives, the people around us may become uncomfortable. Some of our so-called friends may become like arsenopyrite, they will become 'cool' towards us. They will stop calling, socially 'ice' you out, or shun you. When they start 'cooling' they release their toxins by encourage others to shun you because you have 'changed'. Other arsenopyrite 'friends' may have an opposite reaction and get 'hot' when they see you are making changes in your life that outshine them. They will try to 'burn' you by making hurtful, negative comments to damage your self-esteem. They will release toxins causing poisonous reactions of self-doubt, fear, and anxiety. The arsenopyrite 'friends' will always act as if their intentions are 'golden', when in fact they are poisonous and damaging. Are you in a toxic relationship with 'arsenopyrites'?

Here are a few red flags to look for:

- Everything is always about them
- They are highly critical of everything that you do
- They betray your trust
- You feel stressed when you are about to be around them
- You feel relieved after they leave
- They can't see their own flaws

- They must always be right

Those are just few warning signs that your friendships with people that exhibit such behaviors are toxic and nothing more than 'fool's gold'. **If you are to aspire to greatness and make your vision a reality, you have to remove the arsenopyrite-type people from your life.**

(R) REINFORCEMENT

Last but not least in the V.A.P.A.R model is reinforcement – as you move powerfully and courageously in living your best life you may suffer setbacks. Positively Reinforcing your VISION, AFFIRMATIONS, PLAN, and ASSOCIATES will keep you on track! Remember to let others cheer you on and when you need help getting back on the right path…. stop call and let someone walk beside you. Do not feel like the driver of the car wandering aimlessly letting others dictate your life. Take control with V.A.P.A.R so you can Aspire to Your Greatness!

Aspire to Your Greatness!

1. Plan for your greatness. (Don't just wait for it to happen, create a plan to support you in getting there.)
2. Use the power of visualization to support you.

3. Use affirmations to bring forward what matters to you and to become all that you are called to be.

4. Have a plan! And then follow the plan.

5. Pay attention to who you associate with. Be mindful of those around you and choose wisely.

6. Reinforce your vision, re-align with your goals, and be willing to get back on track towards your greatness.

7. Aspire and Step into your Greatness!

CHAPTER 10 – ASPIRE TO YOUR GREATNESS!

As a young girl, I had to learn how to rise above prejudice, discrimination, and the abusive actions of others towards me. I was taught that **Life is Not Fair,** but what I would learn is that I need not become a helpless victim of my circumstances, but instead choose to be an empowered survivor that would rise above the challenges that life presents and learn from them.

As I blossomed into a young woman in **Wildflower,** I learned that in difficult situations, when we are most vulnerable, afraid, and feeling hopeless, we are more powerful than we could ever could imagine. For example, when I was homeless and faced uncertainty about my future. My biggest challenge was not fixing the problem, it was believing that I had the capabilities to make it on my own, especially after being told otherwise. We have capabilities, talents, and gifts that may be lying dormant like seeds deeply embedded within us that do not come forth unless we are faced with storm-like trials. Our abilities, like those seeds will sprout, as we face trials in our lives, grow as we overcome the obstacles, resulting in a blossoming effect as develop into better versions of ourselves.

Another lesson that I had to learn was to be true to myself, stop trying to please others and listen to my inner wisdom. **Everybody that is in your circle, is not in your corner,** helped me to appreciate the importance of removing toxic people from my life. Admittedly, it was a painful process. We want to assume that people really care for us and want the best for us, but it would be wise to follow the advice of Dr. Maya Angelou, 'when people show you who they are believe them'. In the process, self-evaluation was critical for me to ensure I had not adopted any of the emotional draining traits of people that needed to be eviscerated from my close circle of friends. A few questions I had to ask:

- Does this person generally speak negative about other people? If so, it is highly likely they are treating me the same way behind my back.

- Does this person exhibit happiness for the successes and accomplishments of others?

- Does this person always feel the need to compare themselves with you, correct you, or put down your opinion on matters?

- Does this person threaten to end the relationship every time things don't go their way?

- Does this person show they care about you only when it is convenient for them?

That leads me to the next lesson about the company we keep. Are we limiting ourselves because of the people around us? We have talents and gifts that if tapped into could elevate us to new heights so we can soar, but we refrain from doing so because we have adopted the mindset of the people around us that are not interested in reaching new heights or stretching themselves for something greater. This lesson helped me to appreciate how important it is to surround myself with people that are soaring to new heights.

Fail to plan, plan to fail – no goals, no strategy, no direction, no purpose is a life without fulfillment. I learned that is important to live with purpose. We are not here by accident. We have a purpose, so we should not live our lives by accident as it were, but **Live on Purpose.** We can make our dreams become a reality when we live with a clear purpose and have a plan of action.

The ones we love also factor into our lives and its purpose. We protect the ones that we love, sometimes at great cost, but do so with reservation or regret. There are numerous accounts of mothers performing extraordinary acts to save children, such as lifting a car, running into a burning building, and jumping into raging floodwaters to save her precious children. She has the strength of Mama Bear and the courage of fearless lion under attack. A lion's family is called its pride. If we think of our family as our *pride*, we would do whatever necessary to **Protect our Pride**.

If love is the bond to keep people together, forgiveness is an oil or healing balm to help soothe friction and heal wounds. It can serve as a bridge over troubled waters or **Stepping Stones** across waters that were once considered in navigable. In the words of Daphne Rose Kinma, "Holding on is believing that there's a past; letting go is knowing that there's a future", we need to let go of anger, resentment, and bitterness and step into the future of peace and contentment.

I learned the beauty, depth, and power in forgiveness and having an open heart, even when the heart had been broken or wounded. It is not only time that heals wounds, but it's forgiveness that has the regenerative power to restore a relationship and make it better than it was before the trauma or injury. I shared with you the physical and emotional pain inflicted upon me as a child by my mother that left me bitterly resenting her. Those negative emotions took a toil upon my health. I was diagnosed with chronic fatigue syndrome when I was twenty-two years old suffered from debilitating migraines throughout my late teens and early twenties. I was a regular visitor at the doctor's office being prescribed one drug after another as searched for relief. I didn't find relief until I learned to forgive my mother and stop looking at our relationship as something that was irreparable. The relationship was dormant, but not dead, it could be resuscitated. What do I mean? A plant can look dry and withered making someone believe that it is dead. Actually, the plant, may just be dormant because it's stressed from its environmental conditions. It becomes dormant for self-preservation as it awaits more suitable conditions for sustainability. The relationship with my mother was stressed and the environment was highly toxic, leading to a dormant relationship that appeared dead, but I learned as an adult, at the root there was love. Over the years, the roots came out of hibernation, and within a nurturing, loving environment it allowed our relationship to grow and blossom. The fruitage? As of today, my mother is one of my closest friends and one that I hold most dear in my heart. We chat on phone every day like two longtime girlfriends. We work together in her travel business and have fun traveling together. She takes my children on trips around the world. She is my biggest cheerleader and advocate, beaming with pride as she shares stories and photos of me. Our relationship has made me a believer in the power and beauty of forgiveness. I can now say, I am blessed with a loving mother, amazing grandmother, and wonderful friend.

On this life journey of self-discovery and learning, I am helped to appreciate that as much as I know there is still so much more that I don't know. On my **Journey to Better**, I keep seeking ways to become a better 'me' without losing sight of my values and who I am. What has helped me on my journey is having a map, or a **Plan to Greatness** that helps me stay focused, motivated, and determined to do and give my best every day.

Rome was not built in a day. Someone will say this to an impatient person that wants to see a rapid turnaround or results in an unreasonable time frame. In our lives there might be times that we want to see rapid results. Just remember a mighty empire of Rome did not start that way. It started out as a settlement, later a city, and later expanded into an empire. How? Brick by brick. When the first bricks were being laid, no one celebrated the growing settlement. As bricks were being added, it might have been noted by local villages, but still there wasn't any grand scale praise for the expansion. The hard work was being done without much fanfare and despite the lack of recognition, the work continued. There was no applause. Many times, there were setbacks. There was internal and external fighting, but the work continued, brick by brick.

Greatness does not happen overnight. You will work hard. When you start a business or take your life in a new direction, you will make many sacrifices that most people won't see. As you lay the 'bricks' and build your business and new life, just remember that Rome was not built in a day. There will be times you will want to give up. You will have to stay focused on your dream even when you have exhausted all your resources. That is when the internal forces within speak the loudest and the fight is the hardest. **Don't give up! You will have to face external forces that will encourage you to take it easy or give up on your dream. Don't give up! Keep laying bricks!**

Are you just a bricklayer or an empire builder? Does it matter? Two bricklayers were interviewed and here is what they had to say about their work. The first bricklayer complained that he was virtually a slave. Nothing more than an underpaid laborer who spent his days wasting his time, placing one brick on top of another for hours on end. The other bricklayer had a different outlook. "I'm the luckiest person in the world! I get to be a part of very important, useful, and beautiful pieces of architecture. I turn simple pieces of brick into exquisite masterpieces."

Do you see the difference? The two bricklayers were doing the same job, but had a different mindset. As you work toward realizing your dreams, reaching goals, and living your purpose, do your best to have the mindset of the bricklayer that looked at his work as something useful, purposeful, and remarkable. **You are making a difference! Just remember, Greatness doesn't happen overnight.**

My dream for you is to remember you are an empire builder! Remember to be willing to take the steps and aspire (and step into) your greatness!

ABOUT THE AUTHOR

Adrian Jefferson Chofor, a global mobility lifestyle expert, life mastery strategist, and transformational speaker founded Aspire2Inspire Transformational Practice, LLC, a heart-centered practice to get people to Strategize, Energize, and Maximize opportunities for attaining goals and reaching fulfillment in their personal and professional lives. The former expatriate, serves as a strategic thinking partner for organizations and individuals faced with multicultural challenges. She strategically equips her clients with tools and resources to ensure a successful transition into living and working in an international environment.

Her mission is to help others make emPOWERed moves to live the life they want by transitioning out of careers they have outgrown and create career opportunities doing the work they have always wanted to do while living in a place they have always wanted to live, and be the person they always wanted to be.

Adrian has co-authored two books: *"Step Forward and Shine!"* an international bestselling book and *"Empowering YOU, Transforming Lives"*. She has been a contributing writer to the RHG Magazine & TV Guide. She plans to launch her own podcast early 2019. She lives in the Bay Area, northern California with her husband and two adorable children. She is available for speaking engagements, group workshops or private consulting. Connect with Adrian at www.adrianjeffersonchofor.com.

Email: connect@adrianjeffersonchofor.com

Facebook: https://www.facebook.com/adrianjeffersonchofor

Facebook: https://www.facebook.com/**expat2go**

Twitter: https://twitter.com/**expat2Go**

REVIEWS

Trisha Garrett

"An extraordinary book where you will experience healing, self-love, resilience, determination, hope and the incredible power of forgiveness, which brings new life! Adrian's passion to impact lives is evident at the end of each chapter as she provides succinct guidance for the reader. Aspire to your Greatness is definitely a MUST read!"

~Trisha Garrett
Founder, CEO Life You Deserve
Best Selling Author, International Speaker
www.LifeYouDeserve.com
FB: http://www.facebook.com/trisha.garrett77

Olivia Parr-Rud

"If you feel called to step into a greater expression of yourself or aspire to share more of your unique gifts then this truly amazing book is a must read. As a survivor of many of life's most extreme challenges, Adrian Jefferson Chofor is my heroine. In every difficult situation, she finds some thread of hope that pulls her through and builds a repertoire of wisdom and strategies that empower you to "Aspire to Your Greatness." She also demonstrates the power of gratitude for those who helped her see her beauty and recognize her enduring strength and wisdom. And most admirably, she models true compassion and caring for those who didn't support her – a wonderful lesson for all of us. If you have any excuse for not following your dreams or feel like life's circumstances are holding you back, then this book is for you."

~Olivia Parr-Rud, MS
Corporate Love Ambassador
LOVE. Make it your business.
https://www.facebook.com/LoveMakeItYourBusiness/
Certified Holacracy Practitioner
610 563-8866 (Mobile)
215 948-3500 (Office - message only)

Linda F. Patten

Aspire to Your Greatness is written from story in a very powerful way. Author Adrian Jefferson Chofor tightly weaves her own story to the lessons she imparts about her journey to greatness, and how we can take that same journey ourselves. The stories are poignant; they are touching; they are joyous, and they are inspirational. I had a hard time putting the book down as I wanted to keep going to know what would be revealed next. Adrian provides notes at the end of each chapter to remind me of the important and key teachings for my own journey to greatness.

~ Linda F. Patten, Leadership Trainer for Women
Entrepreneurs and Changemakers – President &CEO,
Dare2Lead With Linda,
Website: www.dare2leadwithlinda.com,
email: linda@dare2leadwithlinda.com

website: www.dare2leadwithlinda.com
https://www.facebook.com/dare2leadwithlinda
https://www.facebook.com/linda.patten.311
https://twitter.com/patten_linda
https://www.linkedin.com/in/lindapatten
http://www.youtube.com/c/LindaPatten
https://plus.google.com/+LindaPatten
https://www.pinterest.com/lindapatten311/

Rebeca Gelencser

Allowing ourselves to be great, can be daunting. I have never seen a female entrepreneur embrace their vulnerabilities in such a powerful way and becoming unstoppable as they inspire other women to fight for their emotional and financial freedoms. Adrian has mastered the art of leveraging her weaknesses and shows the readers how to transform their limitations into strengths in this book. Adrian reminds us that greatness is planned and that a plan is only as good as those that see it though. This book is a work of art!

~Rebeca Gelencser
Career Coach
Skype: rebeca.gelencser (valenca)
Webpage: http://rebecagelencser.com/
https://www.linkedin.com/in/rebeca-gelencser/
Tel: +41 76 495-4144

Marlene Elizabeth

If you've ever heard the saying, "*do something today that your future self will thank you for*" reading Dr. Adrian Jefferson Chofor's book **IS** that something! A beautifully written, deeply tender, inspiring story of healing and transformation of a native New Yorker. From a harsh childhood that leads to homelessness, to 9/11 and rich European travels, this book is filled with powerful stories, miracles, answered prayers, forgiveness, courage and valuable life lessons. You'll laugh, cry and cheer but most of all, you'll see you already have everything you need to aspire to your greatness!"

~Marlene Elizabeth
Certified Money Coach®
and Bestselling Author of MONEYWINGS™
Website: www.GrowMoneywings.com
Email: Marlene@MarleneElizabeth.com
Facebook: https://www.facebook.com/growmoneywings/

Sheena Walker

WARNING

Do not read this book unless you want to Aspire to Greatness
Forget ABOUT being the ugly duckling
Forget being around people who abused you physically and
mentally
Forget the cardboard box on the street you slept in

Forget been in the rat race that stole your identity.

Discover how Adrian brilliantly shares a step-by-step guide to
"Aspiring Greatness now "
In this book you will learn how Author Adrian went from a life
of abuse and homelessness, challenges beyond the
unthinkable, to living the life of her dreams.
Discover how Adrian brilliantly describes how her bold moves
led to her achieving big dreams.

Through sheer grit, determination and bounce- back ability,
Adrian went from zero to being a hero to celebrate success in
her life.

Learn how to diminish the size of your but, to YES, I CAN.

Discover how Adrian dealt with the TWIN TOWER tragedy
on that fateful day on September 11.

What a fantastic great read if you want to drastically improve your life and do whatever you want, Adrian SHOWS you how

~Sheena Walker BA

International Business growth Speaker Trainer & Educator of High Performance

Specialist in Public Speaking & World class Presentations skills for entrepreneurs and Business professionals to take Centre Stage

Cynthia Stott

Aspire to your Greatness! is like a movie that unfolds page after page. Adrian Chofor's life story is riveting. I literally couldn't put it down! From homelessness, to living abroad, to becoming a mother...Every chapter more exciting than the next. My favorite part is at the end of each chapter, when she sums up the steps she took to transform and the life lessons she learned along the way. Her pearls of wisdom support every step in your transformational journey.

~Cynthia Stott

International Speaker Coach/Global Visibility Influencer

www.CynthiaStott.com

Programs@CynthiaStott.com

415.298.7306

Monique McCoy

Inspiring and revealing! Adrian Jefferson Chofor writes, "Aspire To Your Greatness", a guide to conquer life's unexpected twists and turns. In my opinion, this is the perfect gift for your close friends and colleagues who need that extra push. It's packed with real life stories and sealed with thought-provoking questions and affirmations. It's also an easy read which is key in a busy world full of distractions!

-Monique McCoy

Author and Transformational Speaker

www.itzmorning.com

Mary E. Knippel

Adrian deftly weaves together the many strands of her difficult life and joins them into parables to teach us that the very words we speak are affirmations. These heartfelt lessons of courage, compassion, and grace offer readers the path to achieve their own greatness!

Mary E. Knippel
Writer Unleashed, Author, Speaker and founder
of YourWritingMentor.com
https://yourwritingmentor.com
http://yourwritingmentor.com
http://fb.com/maryeknippel.author
 San Francisco Writers Conference- Independent
Editor Coordinator
Polka Dot Powerhouse Advisory Board
Co-Author **The Write Nonfiction Now Guide
to Creativity and Flow** (2016)
Co-Author **Come Out of Hiding and SHINE** (2016)
Co-Author **Bloom Where You are Planted
and SHINE** (released Sept. 2017)
Co-Author **Grandmother Legacies**
Co-Author **Step Forward and SHINE**

http://yourwritingmentor.com for free blog writing trigger tips and to grab your complimentary Unleash Consultation.

Kari Kelley

Aspire to your greatness is written so that I felt a part of the story. I could feel the emotions and I could almost see the people that were in each event. I looked forward to the tips at the end of each chapter and I felt like I had a personal guide giving advice and encouragement to Aspire to my greatness. I feel that I will read and share like a life guide to refer to when challenges arise.

Kari Kelley (k2)

Twitter https://twitter.com/Karionk2
Linkedin https://www.linkedin.com/in/kakelley?trk=hp-identity-name
Facebook: https://www.facebook.com/voicesofresilience/